The Greatest Minds in Psychology

METRO BOOKS
New York

An Imprint of Sterling Publishing Co., Inc.
1166 Avenue of the Americas
New York, NY 10036

ISBN 978-1-4351-6304-1

For information about custom editions, special sales, and premium
and corporate purchases, please contact Sterling Special Sales at
800-805-5489 or specialsales@sterlingpublishing.com.

Manufactured in China

2 4 6 8 10 9 7 5 3 1

www.sterlingpublishing.com

Credits: Illustrations by Eva Tatcheva
Design by Elwin Street Productions Limited

The Greatest Minds in Psychology
50 Ideas That Changed the World

Jeremy Stangroom

METRO BOOKS
New York

Contents

Introduction

The word "psychology," derived from the Greek words "psyche" (soul or mind) and "logos" (knowledge or study), means literally "the study of the mind." Although the term first gained general usage in the eighteenth century, it wasn't until the end of the nineteenth century that it began to be used in its modern sense to refer to a distinct domain of inquiry that aims at the scientific understanding of human thought and behavior.

In the present day, under the rubric of psychology, researchers investigate phenomena as diverse as learning, perception, attention, memory, personality, aging, prejudice, obedience, mental illness and human flourishing. In this book, we'll touch on all these topics through the ideas and work of fifty of the greatest psychologists ever to have lived, each one of whom has made a significant contribution to the body of knowledge that constitutes modern psychology.

The history of psychology is in large part the history of its great experiments, and this is reflected in the pages to follow. We're interested in psychology as a living, breathing endeavor, in the research that led to breakthroughs in our understanding of mind and behavior.

It is often the case that psychologists, like most of us, live unremarkable lives, and their legacy to the discipline lies solely in the body of research they bequeath to their colleagues. But there are exceptions. The luminaries in the field—James, Freud, Jung—led remarkable lives, and conjured up ideas and theories that have had a far-reaching cultural and social impact, changing the way we see ourselves and our place in the world. These few rare geniuses stand out, not because their prominence diminishes the importance of their less celebrated colleagues, but because their ideas and work exemplify how the concerns of psychology have an abiding human significance.

1750	
1800	**Pierre Cabanis**
1850	
1860	**Wilhelm Wundt** *The Velocity of Thought* (1862)
1880	**Sir Francis Galton** *Inquiry into Human Faculty and its Development* (1883)
	William James *Principles of Psychology* (1890)
1900	
1903	**Ivan Pavlov** *The Experimental Psychology and Psychopathology of Animals* (1903)
1904	**Edward Thorndike** *Introduction to the Theory of Mental and Social Measurements* (1904)
1910	
1920	
1925	
	John Watson *Psychological Care of Infant and Child* (1928)
1930	**Edward Tolman** *Purposive Behavior in Animals and Men* (1932)
1935	
	B. F. Skinner *The Behavior of Organisms: An Experimental Analysis* (1938)
1940	**Max Wertheimer** *Productive Thinking (1942)*

From Beginnings to Behavioral

The discipline of psychology had its beginnings in the nineteenth century as the human mind increasingly came to be seen as an object worthy of systematic study. In this section, we consider the work of early introspective psychologists such as Wilhelm Wundt, and trace the emergence of psychology as a distinct field of inquiry through the ideas of the first behaviorist psychologists.

The Birth of a Science

Human beings have been interested in the workings of the mind for almost as long as they have been documenting their interest in anything. The ancient Greek philosopher Aristotle, for example, wrote a treatise on the psyche (or soul), in which he discussed, among other things, the character of sense experience, thinking, and the imagination.

However, until modern times, discussion of the mind tended to be highly speculative in character, and was generally considered to fall under the remit of philosophy. The emergence of psychology as a distinct discipline occurred only in the latter part of the nineteenth century, with the opening of Wilhelm Wundt's psychological laboratory in 1879, and with the concomitant drive to put the investigation of the mind on a scientific footing.

Wundt and his colleagues employed the technique of introspection, which involves directing attention toward one's own conscious experience in order to investigate the fundamental structure of conscious thought. Introspection took place in a laboratory setting, and careful efforts were made to ensure that extraneous variables, such as delivered instructions and the character of a given stimulus (e.g., the ticking of a metronome), were held constant. In this way, they hoped the results of introspection would be unaffected by the particular setting in which an experiment took place and would accurately reflect the structure of conscious experience.

However, at this time, their method of psychology was not as scientific as the Wundtians might have hoped. The problem was that the technique of introspection does not produce objective, replicable results. If two researchers trained in introspection employ the technique in order to discern how they experience the ticking of a metronome, and then get different results, there is no way of telling who is right. Introspection, by its very nature, is bound up with

"Psychology as the behaviorist views it is a purely objective experimental branch of natural science. Its theoretical goal is the prediction and control of behavior."

individual subjectivity and, therefore, cannot be the grounds upon which a reliable body of knowledge is built.

By the first decade of the twentieth century, rumblings about the unreliability of the technique were beginning to be heard. In particular, the American psychologist John B. Watson, was scathing about introspection. The Wundtian orthodoxy began to crumble in 1913 with the publication of Watson's article, "Psychology as the Behaviorist Views It," in which he argued that psychology should concern itself only with observable behavior. If psychology wanted to put itself on an equal footing with natural science, then it had to replicate the rigor of its methods, which meant concentrating on what could be observed and measured, and abandoning all references to the internal realm of private experiences.

Thus, Watson defined psychology as "that division of Natural Science which takes human behavior—the doings and sayings, both learned and unlearned—as its subject matter."

In the battle between Wundtian introspectionism and Watsonian behaviorism, the latter decisively won the day. Behaviorism quickly became the dominant psychological paradigm for studying human behavior, particularly in North America, and remained so for nearly fifty years. It was only with the emergence of cognitive psychology in the 1950s that behaviorism's dominance began to be challenged.

After training as a doctor of medicine, Pierre Cabanis rose to prominence in late eighteenth-century France as a member of the Ideologues, a group of thinkers committed to the possibility of a "science of man."

Cabanis's signature work, *On the Relations Between the Physical and Moral Aspects of Man*, argues for a broadly materialist understanding of the relationship between mind and body. He believed that biological life is partly distinguished by its ability to have sensations, and that all our thoughts, feelings, and ideas are caused by sensations. Thus, he was well known for his comparison between the brain and the stomach, arguing that just as the stomach is a machine for digesting food, so the brain is a machine for digesting sense impressions, or, as he put it, secreting thought.

Cabanis is by no means a modern figure. Toward the end of his magnum opus, for example, he discusses the issue of how much water a person absorbs while bathing, arguing that the amount is linked to a person's temperament: the less phlegmatic they are, the more water they're going to absorb.

Others of his concerns, however, are more recognizably modern. He espouses a version of the (erroneous) idea that organisms evolve by means of the inheritance of acquired characteristics, and he favors a program of selective breeding to improve the human condition. He posits the existence of an unconscious, which makes its presence felt during dreams (thereby anticipating one of Freud's central ideas). And he rejects the "blank slate" view of human nature, which holds that whatever one finds in the mind has come in from the outside, stressing instead the importance of internal physiological factors such as age, sex, bodily "dispositions," and health.

The work of Cabanis is now only of historical interest. Nevertheless, his attempt to understand the human mind in terms of the workings of an underlying physiology was an important moment in the early development of the science that eventually became psychology.

Born
1757, Cosnac, France

Died
1808, Meulan-en-Yvelines, France

Cabanis's endeavor to understand the brain in physiological terms was an important early moment in the development of a scientific approach to understanding the mind.

Francis Galton
Pioneering Psychometric Testing

The nineteenth-century polymath Francis Galton is probably best known for his advocacy of eugenics—in his terms, the science that "deals with all the influences that improve the inborn qualities of the [human] race." In a sense, this is unfortunate, because his association with the eugenics movement and its deadly history has tainted what is in fact a rich intellectual legacy.

In the field of psychology, Galton pioneered the study of individual differences, in particular creating the first recognizable tests of intelligence. To learn something about memory, he developed a technique of word association. He was the first to make systematic use of questionnaires, and created a number of new statistical techniques that enabled him to interrogate his data more precisely. And he had novel opinions about such things as mental imagery, inheritance, and nature versus nurture.

The tests of intelligence devised by Galton seem rather bizarre by today's standards. They rest on the assumption that a person's overall mental ability will be correlated with their sensory acuity. So, for example, he devised a test to determine how accurately people were able to discriminate between different weights, and another one to measure the ability to detect pitch. In 1882, Galton established a testing center in London, where, for a fee, a person could take a series of such tests and receive a report at the end.

Galton's most famous test of mental imagery involved asking his subjects to conjure up the picture of their breakfast table that morning, and then to report on whether it was clear, detailed, in color, and so on. To his surprise, he found that there was considerable variation in this ability, a result confirmed by the research of later psychologists.

Galton's importance in the history of psychology should not be underestimated. Although he did not inspire a legion of followers in the same way that Wundt did, above anybody else, he showed how psychologists could fruitfully explore the differences between individuals.

Born
1822, Birmingham, England

Died
1911, Haslemere, England

Galton pioneered an approach to psychology that emphasized the importance of the differences between individuals across mental aptitudes such as memory, sensory discrimination, and visual imagery.

Wilhelm Wundt is properly regarded as the founder of the science of psychology. In 1864, he taught the first course in "Physiological Psychology" at the University of Heidelberg; in 1874, his groundbreaking *Principles of Physiological Psychology* was published; and five years later, he established the world's first experimental psychology laboratory at the University of Leipzig.

Wundt believed that the new science of psychology should aim at uncovering the fundamental structures of conscious thought, arguing that the technique best suited to this task was introspection, the process of examining the contents of one's own mind. However, he did not mean the kind of introspection that we all practice in our daily lives, but rather a rigorous, controlled version of it, designed to elicit reliable knowledge about the human mind.

Wundt's general approach can be illustrated with reference to a series of experiments he conducted with a metronome. A standard experiment would involve a highly trained subject, normally one of Wundt's students, focusing their attention on a carefully selected series of clicks, and then reporting back on some particular aspect of their experience—whether they had experienced the clicks disparately or as a unified whole, for example. It would then be possible to vary the speed and rhythm of the metronome to see whether that had an effect on the experience.

It was in the light of his own experiments with a metronome that Wundt developed his tridimensional theory of feeling. He noted that he tended to experience three different kinds of reaction to the metronome: pleasure and displeasure depending on its rhythm; relaxation and tension depending on whether he was waiting for an anticipated click to occur; and calm or excitement depending on the speed of its beat. On the basis of repeated listenings, therefore, he concluded that every conscious feeling will vary along three continuums: pleasantness-unpleasantness; relaxation-tension; and calm-excitement.

Psychologists no longer take Wundt's theory of feeling seriously, but, nevertheless, his place in the history of psychology is assured.

Born
1832, Manheim, Germany

Died
1920, Großbothen, Germany

Wundt was the founder of the world's first dedicated psychology laboratory, and the champion of introspection as the method most suited to the task of uncovering the fundamental structures of conscious thought.

William James is in many ways a contradictory figure. He was reluctant to call himself a psychologist, yet wrote one of the classics of the discipline. He largely eschewed applied research, but established the first psychology laboratory on the American continent. He is probably better known in the present day as a philosopher, and particularly for his advocacy of "pragmatism," but nobody seriously doubts that he is one of the most important psychologists ever to have lived.

James argued that the starting point of psychology is thought or consciousness. However, he rejected the Wundtian idea that consciousness can be broken down into discrete foundational elements—feelings and sensations—arguing instead that it has five distinct characteristics.

First, every thought is necessarily personal, it belongs to somebody. Thus, James argued that the most fundamental conscious fact is that *I* think and *I* feel.

Consciousness is also in constant flux, which means that we can never have the same conscious thought or be in the same conscious state more than once. This point is shown most clearly by the fact that different objects will conjure up quite different thoughts and emotions depending on our mood, the passage of time, and so on.

A third characteristic of consciousness is that it is experienced as a continuous flow, and not as being chopped into little bits. James was aware that there are breaks in consciousness, of course, but argued that the fact that we so easily reconnect with our own conscious past after such a break—perhaps upon waking from sleep, for example—demonstrates its continuous character.

Another attribute of consciousness is that it is necessarily discriminating and selective. We grasp particular aspects of objects by means of a process of emphasizing, accepting, rejecting, and unifying. We do not merely attend passively to the totality of our experience.

Finally, James held that consciousness is also always of an object that is perceived as being separate from itself (what is sometime referred to as the "intentionality" of consciousness).

Born
1842, New York, New York

Died
1910, Tamworth, New Hampshire

James's ideas about the scope and techniques of psychology remain influential to this day.

The Russian physiologist Ivan Pavlov hit upon the phenomenon that led to the discovery of classical conditioning by accident. He was working on canine digestion when he noticed his laboratory dogs exhibiting a curious new behavior. They would begin to salivate whenever he or his assistant entered the laboratory. It seemed they had learned to associate his presence in the laboratory with the imminent arrival of canine snacks.

Pavlov set about testing this conjecture in a systematic fashion by means of an experiment that has since become perhaps the most famous in the history of psychology. He devised a technique for measuring the extent of a dog's salivary secretions, and was able to confirm that food automatically causes a dog to salivate. In other words, he determined that it is a hard-wired fact about dogs that they salivate while eating. In this sense, food is an unconditioned stimulus (UCS) that causes the unconditioned response (UCR) of salivation in a dog.

The interesting question was whether it would be possible to get a dog to salivate by pairing a neutral stimulus—such as the ringing of a bell—with the unconditioned stimulus. Sure enough, Pavlov found that if a bell and food are paired together frequently enough, a dog will begin to salivate as soon as it hears the bell, even if the food is nowhere to be seen. In this situation, the bell functions as a conditioned stimulus (CS) causing a conditioned response (CR) in the dog.

This kind of learning is known as classical conditioning, and its discovery sparked much research that aimed at uncovering its secrets. For example, Pavlov discovered the existence of second-order conditioning, where a CS (e.g., a buzzer) will in effect function as a UCS if paired with a new neutral stimulus (e.g., a black square). He also demonstrated generalization, where a stimulus similar to the original CS—for example, a bell of a slightly different pitch—will also provoke a CR; and discrimination, where a stimulus of a big enough difference—for example, a bell of a very different pitch—will not provoke a CR.

The work of Ivan Pavlov was hugely influential in the first half of the twentieth century, contributing particularly to the rise of the behaviorist school, and even in the present day remains a valuable contribution to our understanding of how learning occurs.

Born
1849, Ryazan, Russia

Died
1936, St. Petersburg, Russia

Pavlov's legacy is assured due entirely to his discovery of classical conditioning, a type of learning that relies on pairing a neutral stimulus—for example, the ringing of a bell—with an unconditioned stimulus—for example, food.

The studies with animals that American psychologist Edward Thorndike conducted in the last few years of the nineteenth century were likely the first laboratory experiments ever conducted in the area of animal psychology.

Thorndike earned his MA at Harvard University in 1897 and became an instructor in psychology at Teachers College at Columbia University in 1899, where he remained for the rest of his career. His subject was animal learning and his most famous experiments involved cats and a puzzle box. The puzzle box was an open-slatted wooden container from which it was possible to escape only by solving a puzzle—for example, by opening a latch and then pulling a lever. The reward for escaping was food. His idea was to see whether, with practice, an animal would get better at escaping from the box.

The first time he placed a cat in the box, its behavior was random and chaotic. The cat eventually escaped, but only as a matter of luck—it just happened to hit upon the right combination of behaviors to solve the puzzle. However, over time, after repeated trials, the cat's behavior became more and more focussed toward solving the puzzle, until eventually it was able to escape as soon as it was placed into the box.

Thorndike argued that his cats manifested trial and error learning. Each successful escape, together with the reward of food, functioned to stamp the correct behavior into the mind of the animal. The cat didn't understand its situation, or experience a moment of insight, it merely became able to reproduce the behavior that would get it out of the box.

He also maintained that a "law of effect" was in play during this kind of learning. This holds that if a behavior in a particular situation results in satisfaction, then the association between the behavior and the situation will be strengthened. In effect, Thorndike had discovered what later came to be known as reinforcement—put simply, anything that increases the likelihood of a behavior occurring—which became a central concept in the arsenal of behavioral psychologists.

Thorndike's reputation is largely tied up with his work on animal learning but he also made significant contributions to other areas of study, including educational psychology and psychometrics.

Born
1874, Williamsburg, Massachusetts

Died
1949, Montrose, New York

Thorndike is renowned for discovering a "law of effect," which holds that if a behavior in a specific situation results in satisfaction, then the association between the behavior and situation will be strengthened.

John B. Watson's advocacy of "behaviorism," the approach to psychology that he is largely credited with having founded, was a reaction against a prevailing orthodoxy at the turn of the twentieth century that was obsessively focussed on conscious experience and that championed introspection as the means by which to uncover its fundamental elements. Watson rejected the methods of the orthodoxy as esoteric and hopelessly unscientific, noting that the typical attitude of a psychologist of this time seemed to be that if their findings were not reproduced, it was because their colleagues were just not proficient enough in the techniques of introspection.

Watson proposed that psychology should discard all references to the contents of consciousness and focus instead on observable and measurable behavior. His aim was to propel psychology in the direction of the other natural sciences, establishing it as an objective, experimental discipline.

Watson's famous "Little Albert" experiment, which he conducted at John Hopkins University in 1920, shows how such a science might proceed as it deals with human learning. Watson began his experiment by establishing that Albert B., an eleven-month old infant, had no particular fear of a white rat. The question that interested Watson was whether it would be possible to inculcate such a fear into Albert.

To find out, he presented the rat to Albert, and then as Albert reached out to pet it, he struck a hammer against a steel bar that was positioned just behind Albert's head. Not surprisingly, Albert reacted with fear and distress to the loud noise. It took just seven repetitions of this process before Albert started to react in fear to the mere sight of the rat. Moreover, Watson found that Albert's fear quickly generalized to other similar stimuli such as a rabbit and a fur coat.

This experiment is now notorious in the history of psychology for its problematic ethics. A particular objection is that Watson did not attempt to "decondition" Albert's fear of the rat. Nevertheless, the "Little Albert" experiment was the first time that a conditioned response had been demonstrated in a human, and it also showed how psychology might proceed without making reference to internal mental states.

Born
1878, Travelers Rest, South Carolina

Died
1958, New York, New York

Watson, the father of behaviorism, was the first to show, through his experiments with "Little Albert," that a conditioned response can be generated in a human being.

23

In 1910, Max Wertheimer was on a train traveling toward Frankfurt when he had the insight that would eventually result in the founding of the new Gestalt school of psychology. He noticed that flashing lights at a train station created the illusion of movement. The significance of this point is that it showed that perception of movement is possible even where there are no moving elements in the visual field.

Although this was already well-known, Wertheimer and his colleagues were able to show how it undermined the "molecular" approach of the Wundtian psychologists. Perceptual experience is not built out of discrete elements, but rather structured by the whole (Gestalt) perceptual field; or as Wertheimer put it, "There are wholes, the behavior of which is not determined by that of their individual elements, but where the part-processes are themselves determined by the intrinsic nature of the whole."

This point can be illustrated by considering how we tend to organize sensory information. Take the following pattern of symbols, for example: ! ! ! ? ? ! ! ! ? ? ! ! ! ? ?. We will tend to interpret it as being made up of three sets of three exclamation marks and two questions mark (rather than some alternative, but equally possible, configuration). According to Wertheimer, this is because we tend to group similar items together when interpreting sensory information.

Another principle of organization is proximity. Imagine hearing the following pattern of sound: click-click-click, pause, click-click-click, pause, click-click-click. We will tend to interpret the click sounds as belonging to three groups of three, rather than as belonging to a larger group that includes a pause, for example.

According to Wertheimer, this shows that we don't build our perceptual experiences by attending to the discrete elements of experience, and then combining them together, but rather we interpret the elements of experience in terms of the whole context within which they appear.

This insight generated a vast amount of activity on the part of the new Gestalt psychologists. According to one commentator, in the twenty-five years following Wertheimer's initial experiments, 114 separate principles of organization were identified.

Born
1880, Prague, Kingdom of Bohemia

Died
1943, New Rochelle, New York

Wertheimer's work was the inspiration for the development of the Gestalt school of psychology, which holds that perceptual experience is structured by the whole (Gestalt) perceptual field.

Like many of his contemporaries, Edward C. Tolman was attracted to behaviorism because of his dissatisfaction with orthodox introspective psychology. However, where he departed from his more radical colleagues, such as John B. Watson, was in seeing a role for cognitive factors in the learning process.

The significance of this point can be understood by considering how a strict behaviorist would view a rat's learned ability to run a maze. The rat would be seen as merely reproducing certain muscular movements that had been "reinforced" by the rewards that had followed its previous successful attempts to navigate the maze. The maze acts as stimulus, and the rat simply reproduces particular individual kinesthetic responses.

Tolman rejected this view as too simplistic, and, together with his colleagues and students, conducted a series of experiments that showed some of the ways it was deficient as an explanation of learning. One of the most notable of these experiments involved a group of rats running a maze under three different conditions. Group 1 were rewarded with food each time they completed the maze, and quickly learned how to escape it; Group 2 were never rewarded for escaping the maze, and consequently spent the whole time running around randomly; Group 3 were not rewarded for the first ten days, and during this time behaved exactly as Group 2. However, after ten days, they were rewarded, which resulted in very rapid learning, allowing them soon to catch up with the rats in Group 1.

This suggests that the rats in Group 3 had been learning about the maze the whole time they were running it, but the learning had remained latent until rewards were introduced. On the basis of this sort of evidence, Tolman argued for the existence of cognitive maps that function to orient an animal in space, thereby allowing it to produce purposive behavior under the right circumstances. It also showed that while reinforcement might be crucial for behavior, it isn't crucial for learning.

Tolman's importance in this history of psychology is as a pioneer of an early form of cognitive psychology at a time when the behaviorists were dominant. In showing that cognitive processes were in play during learning, his work provided an important corrective to the reductionism of strict behaviorism.

Born
1886, West Newton, Massachusetts

Died
1959, Berkeley, California

Tolman's experiments demonstrated that animal learning is not merely a matter of automatic behavioral responses, but rather involves cognitive elements, including cognitive maps that function to orient an animal in space.

27

B. F. Skinner
Discovering Operant Conditioning

B. F. Skinner's behaviorism is built on the simple, yet powerful, idea that if we want to explain the existence of a behavior, then our best bet is to look at its consequences. In essence, this is just a restatement of Edward Thorndike's law of effect. However, in Skinner's hands, the scope of this idea was extended to the point where it effectively encompassed the whole of human behavior.

Skinner's version of this idea was instantiated in his notion of operant conditioning, which refers to the shaping of behavior by the means of rewards and punishments. This idea can be illustrated by considering how a "Skinner box" operates. A rat is placed inside an enclosed box, within which there is a lever, which, if pressed, will immediately deliver a food pellet to the rat. At first, the rat will just run around aimlessly, but eventually it will bump into the lever with the consequence that it will be rewarded with food. This has the effect of reinforcing the behavior that precedes the reward—that is, the lever pressing. In this way, the rat will quickly learn to go straight to the lever in order to secure the reward. Positive reinforcement, therefore, results in the emergence of lever pressing behavior.

Skinner identified other kinds of conditioning. Negative reinforcement occurs when a behavior is strengthened because it leads to a reduction in pain. For example, he was able to train rats to press a lever by wiring it up so that it functioned to turn off a painful electric shock. Punishment can also be used to weaken certain kinds of behaviors, which presumably is the general idea that motivates the use of sanctions—including, sometimes, the infliction of pain—in order to discourage unwanted behaviors in children.

Skinner's behaviorism is undoubtedly radical in its implications. Although, unlike John Watson, he did not deny the existence of the mind, it played no part in his explanation of behavior. As far as he was concerned, almost all behavior is determined by patterns of positive and negative reinforcement. The power of his approach—whatever its limitations—is unquestionable. It is a striking thought that by using techniques of conditioning, Skinner was able to teach pigeons to play table tennis.

Born
1904, Susquehanna, Pennsylvania

Died
1990, Cambridge, Massachusetts

Skinner discovered what is known as "operant conditioning," a form of learning that stresses that behavior is shaped by its consequences, and specifically by its associated rewards and punishments.

1900	
	Charles Spearman "'General Intelligence,' Objectively Determined and Measured" (1904)
1905	
1930	**Cyril Burt** *Study of the Mind* (1930)
	Gordon Allport *Becoming: Basic Considerations for Psychology of Personality* (1955)
1955	
	Donald Broadbent *Perception and Communication* (1958)
1960	
	Raymond Cattell "The Scree Test for the Number of Factors," Multivariate Behavioral Research (1962)
1962	**Hans Eysenck** *Know Your Own IQ* (1962)
	Norman Geschwind & Edith Kaplan "A Human Cerebral Deconnection Syndrome" (1962)
	George Sperling "Visual Thresholds Near a Continuously Visible or Briefly Presented Light Dark Boundary" (1963)
1963	
	Noam Chomsky *Aspects of the Theory of Syntax* (1965)
1965	
	Jerome Bruner *On Knowing: Essays for the Left Hand* (1979)
1980	**Elizabeth Loftus** *Eyewitness Testimony* (1979)
1985	
	Michael Gazzaniga *Mind Matters: How Mind and Brain Interact to Create our Conscious Lives* (1988)
1990	
	Antonio Damasio *Descartes' Error: Emotion, Reason, and the Human Brain* (1994)
1995	
	Benjamin Libet *Mind Time: The Temporal Factor in Consciousness* (2005)
2005	

The Mind and the Person

As psychology matured in the middle part of the twentieth century, its focus shifted from behavior to a concern with the workings and characteristics of the mind. In this section, we focus on cognitive psychology, looking at the work of luminaries such as Jerome Bruner and Noam Chomsky, and comparative psychology, through the work of psychologists such as Raymond Cattell and Hans Eysenck.

Behaviorism and the Cognitive Revolution

Although there is no simple way to define cognitive psychology, the approach is probably best understood in terms of a metaphor drawn from computer science that sees the brain as an information processing system. The brain is not a mere passive receptacle of incoming sensory information, wedded to the task of reproducing learned responses in behavior, but rather an active system that processes and shapes the information it receives. Cognitive psychologists tend to focus on phenomena such as perception, attention, decision-making, memory, and language acquisition, being concerned to elucidate the active role played by the brain in the processes that underpin them.

Cognitive psychology emerged in the 1950s as a result of a general dissatisfaction with behaviorism, which was, particularly in North America, the dominant psychological paradigm at the time. It had become increasingly clear that in focusing exclusively on behavior and the stimulus-response associations that supposedly underpin all learning, behaviorism was unable to account for the complexity of human thought and behavior.

This sort of intransigent reductionism did not go unchallenged even before behaviorism came under sustained pressure from the rise of cognitive psychology. Edward Tolman's work in the 1930s, which demonstrated the importance of "cognitive maps" for learning, and Jerome Bruner's experiments in the 1940s, which showed that perception was a dynamical phenomenon, were early examples of a departure from a strict behaviorist approach.

The beginning of the "cognitive revolution," which within less than two decades saw cognitive psychology supplant behaviorism as the dominant psychological paradigm, is often dated to 1956, a year

> *"A theory that denies that thoughts can regulate actions does not lend itself readily to the explanation of complex human behavior."*
>
> —Albert Bandura

during which a number of events occurred that are considered pivotal to the rise of the information processing approach.

During the summer of that year, a number of academics, including John McCarthy, who coined the term "artificial intelligence," and Marvin Minsky, convened at Dartmouth College to discuss whether machines could be made to simulate intelligence; and, later in the year, at a meeting at MIT, Noam Chomsky presented a paper that contained the ideas that would the next year become his masterpiece, *Syntactic Structures*, which sparked a revolution in our understanding of the relationship between language and cognition.

Also in 1956, Bruner et al. published *A Study of Thinking*, which was the first serious investigation of the cognitive processes underlying concept formation; and George Miller published his groundbreaking paper, "The magical number seven, plus or minus two," which described some of the limits on the human capacity to process information and is now one of the most cited papers in the history of psychology.

In the present day, cognitive psychology permeates nearly all aspects of psychological research. Although its greatest strength still lies in areas such as memory and attention, which naturally lend themselves to an information processing approach, its influence is felt in domains as diverse as cognitive therapy, cognitive development, and social cognition.

Alfred Binet, a French psychologist working at the turn of the twentieth century, is renowned for developing the first genuinely useful test of intelligence, and also, more generally, for championing the cause of individual psychology, which he took to be the study of those properties of the mind that vary from individual to individual.

Binet was motivated to develop his intelligence "scale" by the thought that if it were possible to identify children who were educationally impaired, then they could be helped through the provision of special education.

His approach in this endeavor was wholly practical. He got two groups of children, one normal, the other impaired, to complete a variety of tests, and then looked for those test items that were sensitive to the difference between the two groups, and also to the difference between children and adults. In this way, together with his colleague, Theodore Simon, he was able to develop the thirty tests of increasing difficulty that comprised his original 1905 intelligence scale.

By 1908, he had revised the scale, basing it on the average performance of a normal child at a particular age. Thus, for example, at age three, a child should be able to point to their nose, eyes, and mouth; at four, they should be able to repeat three digits; at eleven, name sixty words in three minutes; and at twelve, repeat seven digits. It was Binet's view that if a child was unable to complete the tasks for the age group two years behind their own, then they were part of the seven percent of the population that would benefit from special education.

Binet was well aware of the limitations of his intelligence scale. He accepted that intelligence was a complex phenomenon—defining it broadly as the ability to adapt to and master one's circumstances—and his test reduced intelligence to a single item only as a matter of expediency. Binet also rejected the view that intelligence was fixed, believing instead that with the right training it was possible for children to improve their level of intelligence. In the present day, Binet's intelligence scale lives on as the Stanford-Binet Intelligence Scales, which has reached its fifth iteration, and is used for clinical and neuropsychological assessment, early childhood assessment, and evaluations for special education placement.

Born
1857, Nice, France

Died
1911, Paris, France

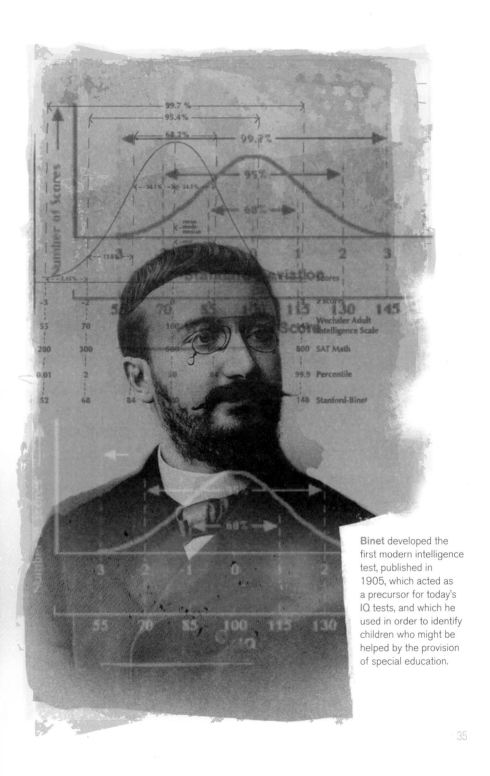

Binet developed the first modern intelligence test, published in 1905, which acted as a precursor for today's IQ tests, and which he used in order to identify children who might be helped by the provision of special education.

Charles Spearman
Identifying a General Factor of Intelligence

The English psychologist Charles Spearman came to psychology relatively late in life after a fifteen-year career in the British Army. However, his tardiness did not prevent him from making breakthrough advances in statistical theory, particularly through his use of factor analysis, nor from identifying a single general factor of intelligence (g), a concept that is still influential in the present day, one hundred years after he originally specified it.

Spearman's discovery of g was the result of an analysis of the patterns of correlation between various common tests of intellectual ability. To put it simply, he discovered that if somebody was good at one kind of test—for example, a test of sensory discrimination—then they also tended to be good at other, seemingly unrelated, kinds of tests (for example, tests of word recall). This suggests the existence of a single factor of intelligence underpinning performance across a range of tests.

According to Spearman, a person's performance on any individual test is a function of this single general factor and also of a factor specific to the particular test. Thus, he argued that intelligence comprises two different sorts of factors: g, the general factor, and s, a multitude of specific factors.

The general factor, which Spearman conceived as having something of the character of a flow of power, is particularly important for those mental operations most commonly associated with reason. In particular, it is dominant for the ability to perceive relations between concepts and for the ability to see how relations in one situation can be transferred to another. Not surprisingly, it is much less important when it comes to abilities that are a long way removed from the operation of reason. For example, it plays virtually no role at all in the ability to distinguish one tone from another.

Spearman's idea of a general factor of intelligence sparked a huge amount of interest and controversy, and is very much a live topic today. Although a number of the criticisms leveled against his particular schema have stuck—in particular the possibility that there might be other general abilities in addition to g—the existence of something akin to his g has good evidential support.

Born
1863, London, England

Died
1945, London, England

36

g

Verbal

s

Mechanical

s

Spatial

s

Numerical

s

Spearman identified a general factor of intelligence (*g*), which he argued underpinned the performance of individuals across a range of tests of cognitive ability.

Upon his death in 1971, British psychologist Cyril Burt was eulogized as one of the discipline's "brightest stars"—the "dean of the world's psychologists," as one commentator put it. His achievements included a British Academy fellowship and more than 350 articles published in a sixty-year career. Six years later, his reputation lay in tatters, destroyed by mounting evidence that he had committed systematic scientific fraud.

Burt's posthumous fall from grace is a complicated story, but in essence he seems to have based his classic studies of monozygotic (identical) twins reared apart (MZAs) on fabricated data in order to bolster his claim that intelligence is largely an inherited phenomenon.

In order to understand what happened, the first thing to note is that the IQ test scores of monozygotic twins are highly correlated. This is exactly what you'd expect if intelligence is largely fixed by a person's genes, but crucially it is also what you'd expect if intelligence is a product of the environment, because twins are almost always brought up together. It is this point that makes monozygotic twins reared apart gold dust to psychologists investigating the heritability of intelligence. If the "hereditarians" are right that intelligence has a large genetic component, then one would still expect the IQ scores of MZAs to be highly correlated.

This is exactly what Burt seemed to have established in three key studies of MZAs, all of which showed that pairs of identical twins reared apart had very similar IQ scores. These studies were considered to be absolutely crucial evidence.

Unfortunately, research by the psychologist Leon Kamin, conducted shortly after Burt's death, uncovered a problem with his data; namely, that it was just too good to be true. Put simply, Burt's three studies reported an identical result, despite the fact they were published many years apart, and despite the final study including three times as many twins as the first study. This is a virtual statistical impossibility, which together with a number of other anomalies, led researchers to conclude that Burt must have fabricated his data.

Not everybody agreed, but what is certain is that the results of Burt's studies cannot now be considered reliable scientific findings.

Born
1883, London, England

Died
1971, London, England

Burt was renowned in his lifetime for his twin studies that seemingly showed that intelligence is in large part a hereditary phenomenon. However, his legacy was tarnished when it came to light that he had fabricated much of his research data.

In 1924, the American psychologist Gordon Allport began to teach a course at Harvard University, titled "Personality: Its Psychological and Social Aspects." Nowadays, there would be nothing particularly unusual about that, but ninety years ago, Allport was a pioneer in the field of personality psychology, and his was the first such course on the American continent.

Allport distinguished between two different approaches to the study of personality. "Nomothetic" approaches focus on the personality characteristics that individuals share in common. So, for example, where people place on a general scale of introversion/extroversion. "Idiographic" approaches, which Allport favored, focus on the uniqueness of every individual, and specifically on the particular traits and dispositions they manifest.

Together with his colleague Henry Odbert, Allport identified approximately 18,000 terms that describe personal characteristics, which he reduced to 4,504 traits proper. Allport suggested a hierarchical organization for the traits that characterize any particular individual. *Cardinal* traits are so all-encompassing that, in effect, they define a person, constituting a ruling passion. Most people, however, do not have a single predominant trait in this sense. Rather, their personalities are built out of *central* traits, which, though few in number, nevertheless constitute the primary mode by which they deal with the world. So, for instance, a person might be generally optimistic, or analytical, or aggressive. Finally, there are *secondary* traits, which are less consistent, and tend to be contingent upon particular situations. Here, we're talking about tastes, preferences, and the like, which might only be known by those closest to the person.

There is a puzzle in Allport's analysis. He claimed that every individual personality is unique, yet the traits he identified seem not to be unique (we all understand what it means to be happy, for example). His way out of this puzzle was to argue that it is the particular configuration of traits that is crucial. Thus, personality in general can be seen as the "the dynamic organization within the individual of those psychophysical systems that determine his characteristic behavior and thoughts."

Born
1897, Montezuma, Indiana

Died
1967, Cambridge, Massachusetts

Allport developed a theory of personality that stressed the uniqueness of every individual, focusing in particular on the configuration of traits that govern a person's thoughts and behavior.

The British-born, American-based psychologist Raymond Cattell is renowned as much for how he conducted psychological research as he is for the discoveries that he made. He pioneered the use of multivariate analysis, which looks at the effect of multiple, interacting variables on thought and behavior, and used complex mathematical techniques, in particular, factor-analysis, in order to draw out the significant patterns in his data.

Cattell's mathematical leanings are strikingly illustrated in the fact that he once conceptualized personality in the form of an equation: $R = f(S, P)$.

This might look complicated but actually isn't. It simply means that a person's behavioral response (R) is a function of the situation they confront (S) and their personality (P). This lines up with his definition of personality as that which tells what a person will do when they are placed in a particular situation.

Cattell's most significant substantive contribution to the discipline of psychology is probably his trait theory of personality. He distinguished between "surface" traits, which are clusters of behavior that tend to be attached to a label in the ordinary language of personality, and "source" traits, which are the underlying building blocks of personality.

Cattell's approach was thoroughly empirical. He started by looking at the 4,504 trait names identified by Gordon Allport, managing to whittle this data down to just 171 traits by discarding synonyms. He then looked at how these traits correlate together, eventually identifying 46 clusters, which constitute surface traits. He argued that these 46 surface traits make up the personality sphere—the total domain of personality traits.

Cattell uncovered the source traits that constitute the structure of personality by performing factor-analysis on these 46 surface traits. This statistical technique, which reduces complex data to a small number of dimensions, allowed him to identify 16 primary factors of personality that explain the way that the surface traits tend to cluster together. These source traits include warmth, reasoning, and emotional stability, and constitute the basis of his hugely influential 16 Personality Factor (16 PF) Questionnaire.

Born
1905, West
Bromwich, England

Died
1998, Honolulu,
Hawaii

Cattell used statistical techniques in order to demonstrate that there are sixteen primary personality factors, including, for example, warmth, reasoning, and emotional stability.

Anxiety

self-control

Extroversion

independence

16PF

%

Jerome Bruner, working in the United States in the years after the end of World War II, is one of the earliest pioneers of cognitive psychology, which moved the discipline's focus away from an exclusive interest in observable behavior.

In a renowned experiment, Bruner tested the hypothesis that our perception of an object would be affected by what he called "behavioral determinants," particularly the social value of the perceived object and the individual need for the (socially valued) object. This is not as complex as it sounds. In essence, Bruner wanted to find out whether our perception of an object would be accentuated—that is, whether it would become more vivid—if the object were socially valued, and, if so, whether this would be affected by the extent to which the perceiver needed the object in question.

Bruner tested his hypothesis by getting two groups of children— one comprising children from affluent backgrounds, the other from poor backgrounds—to estimate the sizes of pennies, nickels, dimes, quarters, and half-dollars, comparing each group against each other and also against a control group that had estimated the size of cardboard gray disks, identical in size to the various coins.

The results of this experiment strongly supported Bruner's hypothesis. The higher the value of the coin, the greater the extent to which its size was overestimated both compared to its actual size and to the control group's estimate of the size of the identical cardboard disk. Moreover, the estimates of the poor group deviated further from the actual size of the coin than the estimates of the rich group. This suggests that perception is not merely a matter of the nervous system responding passively and predictably to incoming sensory stimuli, but rather that it is an active process that is inextricably linked to the "dynamical system that constitutes the person."

Jerome Bruner is rightly considered one of the architects of the cognitive revolution. His legacy includes important work in the fields of cognitive psychology, developmental psychology, educational psychology, and the psychology of language.

Born
1915, New York,
New York

OVERT
BEHAVIOR

PERSONAL
FACTORS

ENVIRONMENT

Bruner, an early
pioneer of cognitive
psychology, conducted
research that showed
that sensation and
perception are
active rather than
passive processes.

The German-born psychologist Hans Eysenck courted controversy from almost the beginning of his career, shaking up the establishment with his attacks on psychotherapy and psychoanalysis, and upsetting liberal opinion with his trenchant views on heredity, race, and intelligence. Although a polarizing character, there is no doubt he made significant contributions to the discipline of psychology, particularly through his work on personality.

Eysenck identified three major dimensions of personality— extraversion-introversion, neuroticism-stability, and psychoticism-impulse control—each of which is associated with characteristic personality traits. For example, extraverts tend to be sociable, talkative, and sensation-seeking, whereas introverts are quiet, reserved, and shy. People high in neuroticism are anxious, moody, and touchy, whereas people low in neuroticism are even-tempered, relaxed, and rational. Individuals high in psychoticism are aggressive and antisocial, whereas those low in psychoticism tend to be warm and empathetic.

Perhaps the most interesting aspect of Eysenck's approach is the thoroughly biological explanation he gave for these different personality dimensions. In essence, he thought that personality is related to innate levels of brain arousal— introverts, for example, have naturally high levels of arousal, whereas extraverts have naturally low levels. This means that introverts are going to reach their optimum level of arousal—the point beyond which any increase in arousal becomes unpleasant—sooner than extraverts. Therefore, introverts will tend to avoid environments and situations that are over-stimulating. Extraverts, on the other hand, struggle to reach their optimum level of arousal, which means they will seek out situations where they can find plenty of stimulation.

Eysenck makes a similar kind of argument for the neuroticism dimension of personality. He argues that neurotics show greater activity in the brain's limbic system, which is responsible for regulating emotional states such as aggression, fear and sex. This makes neurotics more susceptible to stress responses in the face of minor setbacks than emotionally stable people, who have lower levels of activity in the limbic region.

Born
1916, Berlin,
Germany

Died
1997, London,
England

A hugely controversial figure, **Eysenck**'s lasting impact comes from his development of a thoroughly biological theory of personality, which breaks personality down into three major dimensions.

Benjamin Libet, an American neuropsychologist, is best known for a series of experiments he conducted in the 1980s that cast doubt on the idea that the decisions that people make are under their conscious control. The inspiration for these experiments was the discovery that conscious acts are preceded by the build-up of an electrical charge in the brain, a readiness potential, which raises the disconcerting possibility that decisions are merely a function of unconscious brain activity.

To test whether this readiness potential occurs before a person even becomes aware that they're going to act, Libet wired people up to an electroencephalogram (EEG), and asked them to perform a simple task, such as a flick of a wrist, whenever they wanted to do so. They were also asked to record a clock-time associated with their first awareness that they were going to act. This gave Libet three bits of data: the time of the act, the time of the person's awareness that they were going to act, and the time of the appearance of the readiness potential (which was measured using the EEG).

The experiment showed that the readiness potential occurs in the brain some 350 milliseconds before a person knows that they are going to act. This led Libet to the startling conclusion that the "initiation of the freely voluntary act appears to begin in the brain unconsciously."

Libet did not accept that this entirely eliminated a role for the conscious will in the decision-making process. A person's awareness that they're going to act occurs some 150 milliseconds before the act itself. According to Libet, this is enough time for the conscious will to exercise a power of veto over any potential act.

Although Libet thought that the temporal relation he found in the laboratory between unconscious brain processes and voluntary acts would hold in the more complicated decision-making situations of everyday life, he denied that this meant we should give up on the idea of free will altogether. Instead, he argued that non-determined free will was a better scientific option than its denial by determinist theory.

Born
1916, Chicago, Illinois

Died
2007, Davis, California

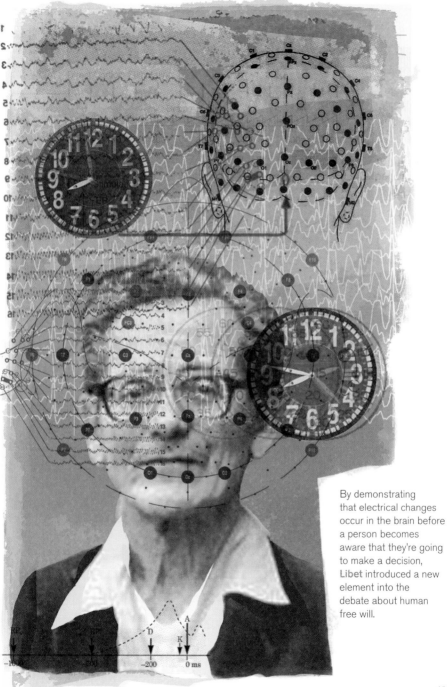

By demonstrating that electrical changes occur in the brain before a person becomes aware that they're going to make a decision, **Libet** introduced a new element into the debate about human free will.

Albert Bandura
Developing Social Learning Theory

Albert Bandura's social learning theory, which he first developed while working at Stanford University in the 1950s, rests on the proposition that learning occurs not only through the effects of one's own direct actions, but also by means of modeling (or imitation). Put simply, we learn by observing others. The 1961 Bobo doll experiment, one of the most famous in the history of psychology, provides strong evidence to support this contention.

Bandura and his colleagues exposed children between the ages of three and six to an adult model—an actor—behaving violently toward a Bobo doll. They hypothesized that this group of children would manifest higher levels of aggression than a control group when allowed to play with a Bobo doll themselves later on. The results of the experiment confirmed the hypothesis; the children exposed to the violent model tended to reproduce exactly the behavior they had witnessed.

Although the basic premise of social learning theory is straightforward, there is complexity in the detail. Bandura identified a number of factors that have to be in place for successful learning to occur. If you want to learn, then you have to attend to the behavior being modeled. You also have to retain the information you have witnessed, which relies on it being codified, and which is facilitated by mental rehearsal. Having retained the information, you have to be able to reproduce it. And finally, you have to be motivated to reproduce the behavior you have learned.

Motivation is key to explaining the distinction between learning and performance. Reinforcement and punishment are important motivators, even when experienced merely vicariously. In a 1965 Bobo doll experiment, Bandura found that children who had witnessed the violent model being reprimanded for his behavior were much less likely to reproduce the violent behavior themselves when playing with the doll later on. According to Bandura, this shows that while reinforcement and punishment are not necessary for learning to occur, they can be necessary for performance. Bandura's social learning theory has been hugely influential. In particular, it has been deployed in order to explore the effects of the media on aggression and antisocial behavior.

Born
1925, Mundare,
Alberta, Canada

Bandura, the originator of social learning theory, challenged the behaviorist model of learning by showing that people can learn simply by observing others.

Norman Geschwind
Exploring the Brain and Mind Relation

Norman Geschwind, an American neurologist, was fascinated by the relationship between higher cognitive functioning—in particular, language—and the underlying neurological processes that govern it. He came to this interest through his work with aphasic patients—people who are unable to formulate and/or understand language—at the Boston VA Hospital, where he was employed as a staff neurologist in the late 1950s. This set the pattern for his career, with many of his most important studies dealing with what happens when the brain goes wrong.

An early study of brain-tumor patient "P. J. K." is characteristic of Geschwind's general approach. The patient was a 41-year-old police officer who had been admitted to the hospital for treatment, where he showed a number of unusual symptoms. For example, if he held an object out of his own sight in his left hand, he could manipulate it in a way that suggested he understood its proper use. However, he would be completely unable to give a correct verbal description of it, or to select it from among a group of objects with his right hand, despite the fact he could later on select it with his left hand and also draw it with his left hand. More generally, he frequently performed verbal commands incorrectly with his left hand, even though he had no such problems with his right hand.

Geschwind, and his colleague, Edith Kaplan, argued that the most likely explanation for this pattern of neurological deficit was a disconnect between the two hemispheres of the brain. P. J. K. was able to accomplish tasks that could be handled autonomously by just one hemisphere, but as soon as a task required a transfer of information between hemispheres, he floundered. Geschwind hypothesized that the cause of this phenomenon was a lesion of the corpus callosum—the brain structure that connects the two hemispheres.

Perhaps the most important general point about this sort of research is that it does more than simply help us to understand how things can go wrong in the brain. Put simply, if we understand neurological dysfunction, then we are at least part of the way to understanding how the brain works when it's functioning normally.

Born
1926, New York, New York

Died
1984, Boston, Massachusetts

Geschwind studied the relationship between higher cognitive functioning and the underlying brain processes that govern it by looking at what happens when the brain goes wrong.

The British psychologist Donald Broadbent was at the center of the move away from behaviorism that occurred within academic psychology in the middle part of the twentieth century. In particular, his groundbreaking studies of attention, a topic that had been largely ignored for fifty years, were indicative of a burgeoning interest in the way that the mind acquires, processes, and stores information.

Broadbent's major research interest was selective attention, which refers to our ability to concentrate on particular pieces of information, while filtering out all nonrelevant material. Together with Colin Cherry, he developed dichotic listening as a procedure with which to study this phenomenon. This technique involves presenting a subject with two competing streams of auditory information, one sent to each ear via a pair of headphones, and then asking them to attend to just one of the streams, and to repeat it aloud as soon as they hear it—a practice termed "shadowing."

Experiments conducted in the 1950s using this technique, showed that we process very little of the non-shadowed information. We might be able to identify whether the speaker is male or female, but we won't be able to say what they're talking about or even whether their message has been reversed.

Broadbent proposed an early filter model of selective attention to account for this phenomenon. He argued that if the brain were able to process every input before selection, then there would be no reason for selection to occur at all. Therefore, the fact that it does occur is evidence that the brain is a "limited capacity channel," where the utility of a selection system is that it produces an economy in mechanism. Selection occurs through the operation of a filter that uses the gross physical characteristics of an input—for example, its spatial location—to isolate it for further processing, discarding everything else. The filter passes the selected input onto the limited capacity channel, where it is processed for content and meaning.

Broadbent's model is a very early attempt to understand the brain as an information processing system. The emergence of new evidence has cast doubt on his specific claims; however, there is no doubting the influence of his general approach, which is an early example of what is now known as cognitive psychology.

Born
1926, Birmingham, England

Died
1993, Aylesbury, England

i
N
P
U
t

sensory buffer

short **term**
memory

Broadbent's early
filter model of selective
attention proposed that
the brain is a "limited
capacity channel"
that discards much
of the information that
comes into it
via the senses,
before processing
what remains.

Noam Chomsky
Discovering a Universal Grammar

In his celebrated work of linguistic theory, *Syntactic Structures,* published in 1957, Noam Chomsky took on the then dominant behaviorist theory of language acquisition, which held that children develop language as a result of training and experience, arguing instead that humans are born with an innate ability to understand the principles that underpin the structure of language.

In its detail, Chomsky's theory is dauntingly complex; however, it is possible to get a general sense of how it works. The first point to understand is that language operates at two different levels. Consider, for example, the following phrases: "The cat hissed at the mouse"; and "The mouse was hissed at by the cat." These phrases have a different surface structure, but at the level of their deep structure—the level of meaning—they are identical.

Chomsky argues that humans have an inborn ability to move easily between these two levels of language. We are able to construct novel, but meaningful, sentences, because we are able to transform deep structure (the level of meaning) into surface structure (the level of particular utterances). The precise mechanism of this transformation relies on a "transformational grammar" that allows people to convert the meaning of what they want to say into particular words and phrases. Put simply, our linguistic ability is built on the set of innate, universal, abstract rules that make it possible for us to move back and forth between the surface and deep structures of language—that is, between the level of specific utterances and the level of meaning.

The evidence for something like Chomsky's view is persuasive, not least because the alternative conception, that language acquisition proceeds by means of the selective reinforcement of correct linguistic performance, is unconvincing given that the number of sentences to which children are ever exposed is but a tiny fraction of the number they are able to generate.

Chomsky's ideas about transformational grammar, though perhaps not in their detail a majority view, revolutionized linguistics in the second half of the twentieth century. Although in the present day, Chomsky is better known for his social commentary, there is no doubt that it is for his contributions to linguistic theory that he will be remembered.

Born
1928, Philadelphia, Pennsylvania

Chomsky argued that our linguistic ability is rooted in an innate ability to transform the deep structure of language, the level of meaning, into particular words and phrases.

George Sperling, an American cognitive psychologist, came to prominence in the early 1960s as a result of a study that demonstrated the existence of what is now called "iconic memory"—a fast-decaying store of visual information.

Sperling's groundbreaking study set out to answer the question, "How much can be seen in a single brief exposure?" By "brief," he meant very brief—imagine, for example, a lightning flash illuminating a scene that you are required to describe. The interest of the question lay partly in the fact that, when asked to report what they had seen during such a brief exposure, people claim to have seen more than they are able to report. This raises the possibility that we have information very briefly available to us that we're not able to report on because it decays too quickly.

Sperling explored this possibility by means of a cleverly constructed experiment that he conducted in 1960. He exposed people to a grid comprising three rows of three letters for a mere 20 milliseconds, and then asked them to recall the letters. On average, his subjects were able to recall about half of the letters, which was in line with the findings of previous research. However, his innovation was to run the experiment again, this time adding in an audible tone, which signaled which row the subject had to recall. The results improved dramatically, with few mistakes being made, which showed that all nine letters are available for recall, but only for a very brief period of time.

An interesting question here is: "just how brief is the duration of our iconic memory?" Sperling tested this by delaying the tone that signaled which row had to be recalled. He found that with a delay, accuracy of recall drops off very quickly. If the tone is delayed by as little as one second, then performance is no better than when the subjects are asked to recall the whole grid.

In the years since his discovery of iconic memory, Sperling has continued to work within the domain of physiological psychology, motivated by a desire to "apply the quantitative and theoretical methods of the hard sciences to the analysis of cognitive processes." In particular, he has developed a number of mathematical models that can be applied to various facets of perception and attention.

Born
1934, New York, New York

Sperling's research led to the discovery of "iconic memory," a store of visual information that human beings are able to access, but only for a very short period of time.

Michael Gazzaniga's pioneering work with split-brain patients in the 1960s and 1970s led him to the radical view that, if conscious unity is disrupted by a fissure between the brain's two hemispheres, you'll get a situation where two minds coexist within the same brain as "two completely conscious entities, in the same manner as conjoined twins are two completely separate persons."

The split-brain procedure, which involves severing a patient's corpus callosum (the band of fibers connecting the brain's two hemispheres), has been performed only rarely, as a treatment for intractable epilepsy. The consequence of the procedure is that the two hemispheres are no longer able to communicate with each other, which provides psychologists with the opportunity to study whether the hemispheres specialize for particular tasks.

The standard experimental technique developed by Gazzaniga (and others, such as Roger Sperry), involves presenting a visual stimulus exclusively to one or the other hemisphere, and then getting the subject to answer questions and/or complete tasks. A striking result of this research is the extent to which the right-hemisphere is deficient in its ability to produce and understand language. For example, if you flash an image to the right-hemisphere, almost inevitably a split-brain subject will say they haven't seen an object (because language is dominant in the left-hemisphere). However, if you then instruct them to retrieve the object using their left hand (which is controlled by the right-hemisphere), they will have no problem in doing so.

The idea that the right-hemisphere has its own distinct mental life, which it is unable to express, is supported by work done with a young patient known as Paul S., who is unique among split-brain subjects in possessing some right-hemisphere language ability. This enabled Gazzaniga and his colleagues to interrogate each of Paul's hemispheres separately. The results were stunning. The two hemispheres appeared to have their own value systems and priorities. Perhaps most striking was the response that each hemisphere gave to a question about a future career. The left-hemisphere indicated that it wanted to become a draftsman, a response that coincided with Paul's earlier expressed wish. But the right hemisphere had a different idea: when instructed to spell out its ideal job, it responded "automobile racer."

Born
1939, Los Angeles, California

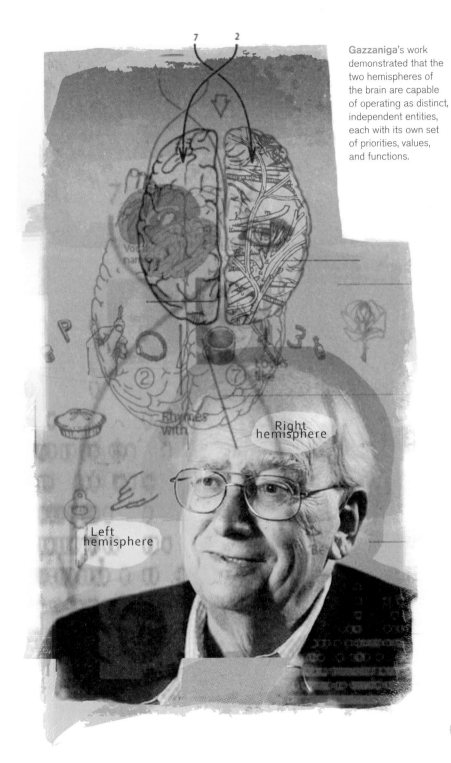

Gazzaniga's work demonstrated that the two hemispheres of the brain are capable of operating as distinct, independent entities, each with its own set of priorities, values, and functions.

Right hemisphere

Left hemisphere

The Portuguese-born neuroscientist Antonio Damasio has spent a large part of his career exploring the relationship between brain, emotion, and rationality. In particular, he is noted for developing a "somatic marker hypothesis," which holds that emotion, and its biological substrate, underpin the ability of humans to make rational decisions.

The most compelling evidence to support this hypothesis comes from Damasio's work with brain-damaged patients. The case of "Elliot," which Damasio discusses in his 1994 book, *Descartes' Error*, is particularly striking.

Elliot's problems began after an operation to remove a brain tumor resulted in damage to his ventromedial prefrontal cortex. Prior to the surgery, Elliot had been a successful businessman, but afterward, his life rapidly began to unravel because he could no longer make even simple decisions. He was unable to dress himself in the morning because he couldn't decide what to wear; it took him thirty minutes to make a simple appointment; and choosing a place to eat lunch could take him until supper-time.

Curiously, Elliot did not manifest any of the standard cognitive deficits. Damasio reports that he was highly intelligent, articulate, and had a good understanding of social conventions and morality. However, Damasio had noticed that Elliot seemed emotionally flat—in particular, he did not appear to be upset about his own predicament. Further testing confirmed that this was the root of the problem: Elliot was living in a world without emotion.

Damasio argues that emotion is necessary for decision making, because it functions to provide cues that enable people to narrow down the vast range of choices that confront them whenever they make even a simple decision. Thus, for example, Elliot did not instantly know that it would be a good idea to get dressed in the morning, because he had no sense of the embarrassment that would inevitably follow if he didn't make that choice. This meant that in order to make any sort of decision he had to work his way through an impossibly complex decision calculus.

Damasio's view that emotion is central to the decision-making process is no longer particularly unusual among neuroscientists and psychologists. However, it remains a marginal view in wider mainstream culture, where emotion is normally seen as the antithesis of reason.

Born
1944, Lisbon, Portugal

Damasio's "somatic marker hypothesis" holds that emotion is central to the decision-making process, to such an extent that its absence can result in decision-making paralysis.

Elizabeth Loftus

Identifying False Memory Syndrome

The American cognitive psychologist Elizabeth Loftus is generally considered one of the most influential living psychologists. Her research focuses primarily on the ways that memory can fail, and it has been important in shaping how we understand phenomena such as eyewitness testimony and false memory syndrome.

Loftus is the architect of many classic studies, one of the earliest of which features two experiments she conducted with John Palmer that looked at how accurately we remember the details of a complex event such as a traffic accident.

In the first experiment, subjects were shown a number of video recordings depicting a traffic accident, and then asked a series of questions about the events that unfolded. The key question varied in a crucial way. Half the subjects were asked how fast the cars were going when they hit each other; the other half had different words substituted in for "hit"—smashed, collided, bumped, and contacted. The idea was to see whether the language used affected the estimate of speed, and the results clearly showed that it did—for example, the mean estimate for "smashed" was 40.5 mph compared to only 31.8 for "collided."

The second experiment explored the more focussed question of whether language affects memory. The procedure was the same as before, except this time the subjects returned after a week, and answered some follow-up questions about the accident. The key question was, "Did you see any broken glass?" There was no broken glass depicted in the accident, but Loftus predicted that those subjects who had previously been asked the "smashed" question would report having seen glass more often than those who had been asked the "hit" question. Again, this is precisely what the results showed, leading Loftus to conclude that by using the word "smash," the experimenter attached a label to the accident, which had the consequence of causing "a shift in the memory representation of the accident in the direction of being more similar to a representation suggested by the verbal label."

The fact that memories can be affected by external information supplied after the fact is clearly of huge significance if one has to make judgments about the accuracy of a person's recall. It is this sort of real-world consequence that makes Loftus's work among the most significant psychological research conducted in the last fifty years.

Born
1944, Los Angeles, California

Loftus's work showed that people's memories can be affected by information supplied long after the occurrence of the event, a fact that has implications for phenomena such as eyewitness testimony and false memory syndrome.

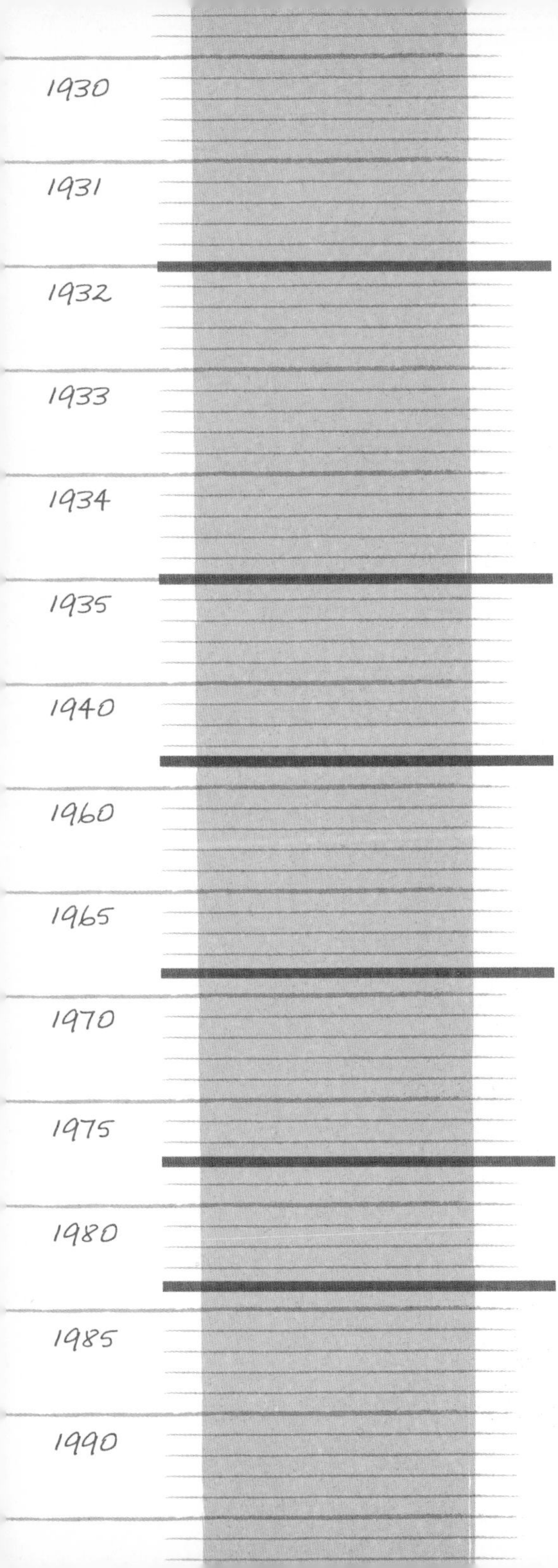

1930

1931

Jean Piaget *The Moral Judgment of the Child* (1932)

1932

1933

1934

Lev Vygotsky *Myshlenie i Rech* (Thought and Language) (1934)

1935

1940

Erik Erikson *Childhood and Society* (1950)

1960

1965

John Bowlby *Attachment and Loss* (1969)

1970

1975

Mary Ainsworth, Mary Blehar, Everett Waters & Sally Wall *Patterns of Attachment* (1978)

1980

Lawrence Kohlberg *The Psychology of Moral Development* (1984)

1985

1990

From Birth to Death

Developmental psychology emerged as a distinct discipline in the 1930s and 1940s. It focuses on the behavioral and cognitive changes that occur in individuals as they move from birth through to death. In this section, we examine the developmental theories of Jean Piaget, Lawrence Kohlberg, and Erik Erikson, and also look at how the psychologists John Bowlby and Mary Ainsworth treated the issue of attachment in young infants.

All in the Genes?

The debate concerning the impact of nature versus nurture (or heredity versus environment) on human thought and behavior is one of the most contentious in the whole of psychology. This is not surprising, because there's a lot at stake. If, for example, it turns out that intelligence is largely an inherited trait, then it raises the possibility that social inequality is written in the genes, and that no amount of education will compensate for a deficit in natural ability.

It is easy enough to identify psychologists who are at the extreme ends of this dispute. Arnold Gessell, for example, one of the earliest pioneers of developmental psychology—which looks at how the maturation process affects thought and behavior—was committed to a thoroughly biological theory of development. Influenced by the ideas of Charles Darwin, he emphasized the intractable impact of genes on the developmental process, denying that parents or teachers could do much to alter its progress.

Gessell believed that the developmental path of an individual, both physical and psychological, is set down before birth. An individual's behavior patterns, personality, and mental capabilities are inherited traits in just the same way as their patterns of physical growth. He did not deny that culture had an impact, but argued that an individual's genetic makeup will determine "how, what, and to some extent even when" they learn.

Contrast this view with the extreme environmentalism of John B. Watson's behaviorist account of learning. He famously claimed that if he were given a dozen healthy infants, and his own specialized world to bring them up in, he could guarantee "to take any one at random and train him to become any type of specialist I might select—a doctor, lawyer, artist, merchant-chief, and yes, even beggar-man and thief, regardless of his talents, penchants, abilities, vocations and race of his ancestors." According to this view, heredity

> "It is in the most unqualified manner. that I object to pretensions of natural equality. The experiences of the nursery, the school, the University ... are a chain of proofs to the contrary."

—Francis Galton

is irrelevant, and learning is just a matter of conditioning the right stimulus-response connections.

We now know that neither of these views is correct. In fact, with particular individuals, it isn't possible to separate out the genetic and environmental aspects of their development. The complexities here are clear in Piaget's famous theory of cognitive development.

Piaget maintained, as we'll see later in this chapter, that humans possess a genetically determined timetable that governs the emergence of particular cognitive abilities. However, the process of development itself is the function of a complex interaction between biological maturation and environmental experience. Put simply, biology provides the apparatus that enables the process of cognitive development, but development only occurs as the individual encounters an environment that poses challenges that need to be solved. Thus, Piaget argued, intelligence consists in a "set of structures constructed by continuous interaction between the subject and the external world."

The issue of nature versus nurture is by no means settled. Although progress has been made in the sense that, in the present day, neither extreme hereditarianism nor extreme environmentalism is seen as a realistic option, the debate about the precise role played by genes and the environment still rumbles on.

Jean Piaget
Investigating Cognitive Development

There is no doubt that the Swiss psychologist Jean Piaget is one of the discipline's standout figures. He is renowned for his work on cognitive development, and particularly for the idea that human intellectual abilities develop according to a genetically determined timetable. It was Piaget's view that children and adults understand and interact with their environment in qualitatively different ways.

Piaget identified four separate stages of development. The sensorimotor stage (0–2 years) is characterized by the achievement of object permanence, which is the awareness that objects have their own separate and independent existence. This is followed by the preoperational stage (2–7 years), during which the child develops the ability to use and manipulate symbols, including language. At this point, the ability to generalize beyond what is immediately given in experience has not yet developed, and the child cannot yet apply logical principles. These abilities begin to emerge during the third, concrete operational stage (7–11 years), during which the child also becomes less egocentric in orientation, in part because they gain an awareness that their viewpoint is only one among many. The final, formal operational stage, which normally starts between the ages of 11 and 15, is characterized by the ability to engage in decontextualized, abstract thought. According to Piaget, almost everybody will achieve this stage of development by the time they are 20 years old.

Piaget argued that intellectual development is driven specifically by a process of assimilation, disequilibrium, and accommodation. The idea here is that a child makes use of behavioral and mental schemas in order to make sense of the world. If a child comes across some genuinely new phenomenon, then they will not be able to assimilate the experience to the existing schema. This results in a state of disequilibrium. The way through this roadblock is to change the existing schema in order to accommodate the new experience, thereby reestablishing a state of equilibrium. It is by this general process of adaptation that intellectual progress occurs. The fact that so many outstanding psychologists, including Vygotsky and Kohlberg, have been influenced by Piaget's ideas is indicative of the extent of his importance to the discipline.

Born
1896, Neuchâtel, Switzerland

Died
1980, Geneva, Switzerland

Equilibration

Disequilibration

Piaget is renowned for his theory of development, which holds that human cognitive maturation occurs in distinct stages, and is governed by a genetically determined timetable.

Lev Vygotsky
Exploring the Social Aspects of Development

The ideas of the Soviet psychologist Lev Vygotsky did not make an immediate impact in the West, partly because he wrote in his native Russian language, and partly because his works were suppressed by the Soviet authorities during the middle part of the twentieth century. It was only in the early 1960s, with the publication of his book, *Thought and Language*, that his work came to wider attention, which makes it remarkable that in the present day, he is second only to Piaget in importance as a developmental psychologist.

Although Vygotsky's work is fragmented and incomplete—a consequence of his premature death at the age of thirty-seven—it is possible to identify a number of key themes and ideas. Perhaps the most important is the claim that cognitive development is thoroughly social and cultural in nature. In particular, Vygotsky believed that the higher mental functions, such as reasoning and language, emerge out of concrete social experience.

His concept of the zone of proximal development (ZPD) is relevant here. He defined this as "the distance between the actual development level as determined by independent problem-solving and the level of potential development as determined through problem-solving under adult guidance." This is not as complicated as it sounds. In essence, the ZPD comprises those skills that exist just beyond a child's cognitive ability, but which they are able to master with the help of a more knowledgeable other, such as a parent or teacher. In this sense, development follows learning: with the right guidance, a child can learn skills that are in advance of their current stage of development.

The process of learning is social not only because it occurs within the context of a social exchange, but also because the mechanisms employed to aid learning are thoroughly embedded within the history of a culture. Thus, for example, Vygotsky noted that we make use of a variety of cultural tools in order to develop our intellectual abilities, the most important of which is language. Vygotsky's ideas are frequently contrasted with those of Jean Piaget. Although both agreed that development occurs as a result of a child's active engagement with the environment, Vygotsky allowed a much greater role for directed learning and the influence of cultural factors.

Born
1896, Orsha, Russia

Died
1934, Moscow, Russia

Vygotsky's theory of development emphasizes the importance of cultural and environmental factors in the developmental process, stressing in particular the role of parents and teachers in facilitating directed learning.

Erik Erikson
Developing the Notion of an Identity Crisis

The German-born, American psychologist Erik Erikson is best known for his stage theory of development, which holds that over the course of a lifetime, human beings will pass through eight psychosocial stages, each of which involves a struggle between two opposing outcomes, one adaptive, the other maladaptive.

The eight psychosocial stages are: trust vs. mistrust (0-1 years); autonomy vs. shame and doubt (1-3 years); initiative vs. guilt (3-6 years); industry vs. inferiority (6-11 years); identity vs. confusion (12-18 years); intimacy vs. isolation (18-35 years); generativity vs. stagnation (35-64 years); and integrity vs. despair (65+ years).

It is possible to get a sense of how Erikson's theory works by looking at the "identity versus confusion" stage, which occurs during the years of adolescence. According to Erikson, the most important challenge of adolescence is to develop a strong sense of personal identity. This involves creating a robust, integrated sense of self, which is normally achieved by developing a clear idea of a future occupation or role in life.

However, the possibility of an identity crisis (a term that Erikson is credited with originating) looms large during adolescence, because the identities forged in childhood no longer suffice as the individual transitions into adulthood. A failure to develop a new identity results in role confusion, which is associated with a number of maladaptive patterns of behavior.

Perhaps most dramatically, role confusion can lead the adolescent to adopt a negative identity, which is marked by abnormal and delinquent behavior. This is an extreme response, but it emerges because even a negative identity is preferable to the alienation and estrangement that results if the adolescent is unable to achieve any coherent sense of identity.

Erikson did not believe that an individual has to meet the demands of each stage before moving onto the next stage of development. However, he argued that failure to achieve a particular adaptive outcome can result in lasting problems. For example, the toddler who fails to learn appropriate levels of trust and autonomy during the first two psychosocial stages might well have trust issues as they move into adulthood.

Erikson's idea that each stage of development requires the resolution of a crisis has proved influential and generated voluminous research, particularly in the area of adolescence studies.

Born

1902, Frankfurt, Germany

Died

1994, Harwich, Massachusetts

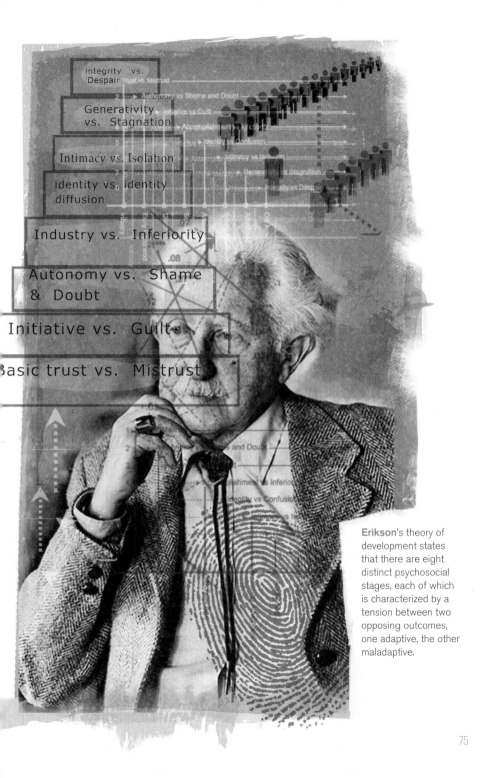

integrity vs. Despair

Trust vs. Mistrust

Autonomy vs Shame and Doubt

Generativity vs. Stagnation

Initiative vs Guilt

Intimacy vs. Isolation

identity vs. identity diffusion

Industry vs. Inferiority

Autonomy vs. Shame & Doubt

Initiative vs. Guilt

Basic trust vs. Mistrust

Erikson's theory of development states that there are eight distinct psychosocial stages, each of which is characterized by a tension between two opposing outcomes, one adaptive, the other maladaptive.

The English psychologist John Bowlby spent the large part of his career studying mothers and their infant children. The result of this work was a theory of attachment that changed the way psychologists think about the mother-child relation, and which threw into sharp relief the harm that can result if the bond between mother and child is disrupted by separation.

Bowlby's theory of attachment is based on the idea that humans are genetically programmed to behave toward their primary caregivers in a way that is likely to secure their own survival. Put simply, evolution has rewarded those behaviors that were successful in keeping the infant close to its caregiver, because those infants were more likely to survive to pass their genes on to future generations.

Bowlby argued that the child is predisposed to form an attachment to just one particular adult—normally, their mother—a tendency he called monotropy. This is achieved most readily in a critical period that begins at about three months after birth and lasts for approximately two years. After this time, if attachment hasn't been achieved, then mothering is next to useless. The consequences of a failure in the attachment process can be profound, resulting in, for example, anxiety, aggression, and delinquency.

Evidence in support of Bowlby's claim that a warm, intimate and continuous relationship with a primary caregiver is necessary for good mental health and emotional stability is to be found in his 1944 study of forty-four thieves. More than half of the young offenders in this study had been apart from their mothers for more than six months during their first five years, compared to only two out of forty-four youths in a non-delinquent control group. Moreover, of the fourteen youths Bowlby identified as manifesting "affectionless psychopathy," a condition characterized by an inability to feel affection and empathy, twelve had spent significant time apart from their mothers as young children.

It was on the basis of this and other evidence that Bowlby famously declared that "a mother's love in infancy is just as important for a child's mental health, as vitamins and minerals are for physical health."

Born
1907, London, England

Died
1990, Skye, Scotland

Bowlby argued that an extended period of separation between a mother and her child during the first years of its life could have dramatic and irreversible consequences for the child's mental wellbeing.

The American-Canadian psychologist Mary Ainsworth is renowned as John Bowlby's major collaborator in the development of attachment theory, and as the architect of the Strange Situation, a procedure devised toward the end of the 1960s that is used to elucidate the different forms of attachment that exist between infant and caregiver.

The Strange Situation was originally devised to examine infant attachment and exploratory behavior in situations of varying levels of stress. The basic setup involves a mother, an infant, and a stranger together in a room with toys. This situation is then manipulated to see how the infant reacts to different kinds of stress. It includes two separation episodes—one where the mother leaves her infant alone with the stranger and one where the infant is left entirely alone; and two reunion episodes, where the mother returns to comfort and settle the infant.

On the basis of the range of behaviors displayed by infants during the Strange Situation, Ainsworth identified three types of attachment. Securely attached infants (70% of all infants) are distressed by the mother's absence, but will explore and play happily if the mother is present. The stranger can provide some comfort, but is not a substitute for the mother. Anxious-avoidant infants (15%) are indifferent toward the mother, and will play happily so long as an adult is present. The stranger is just as able to provide comfort as the mother. Anxious-resistant infants (15%) have an ambivalent attitude toward the mother. They are reluctant to play and explore even while the mother is present, and they are very distressed when the mother leaves. However, although they seek out contact with the mother when she returns, they appear angry and resistant when contact actually occurs. Anxious-resistant infants resist all attempts at interaction by the stranger.

It would be hard to overstate the impact of the Strange Situation procedure on the way that early child attachment has been studied. More than forty years after it was first devised, it is still being modified, criticized, and discussed. More generally, the importance of Ainsworth's research is that it provides persuasive evidence for the broader claims of Bowlby's attachment theory.

Born
1913, Glendale, Ohio

Died
1999, Charlottesville, Virginia

Ainsworth's renowned and influential experimental procedure, the Strange Situation, has provided strong empirical support for the proposition that successful early childhood attachment is essential for the development of trust and feelings of security.

Lawrence Kohlberg
Exploring Moral Development

The American psychologist Lawrence Kohlberg is best known for his stage theory of moral development, which holds that at different stages of intellectual maturity, people will offer different reasons and justifications for the moral judgments they make. To demonstrate this point, Kohlberg developed a number of moral scenarios, including his famous Heinz dilemma.

A woman is dying, and there is one drug that might save her, on sale in a single shop for $10,000. The woman's husband, Heinz, tries to borrow the money, but only manages to secure about half the drug's cost. He goes to the shopkeeper, tells him that his wife is dying, and begs him to sell the drug for less, or to let him pay the balance at a later date. The shopkeeper refuses. The husband is desperate, and breaks into the shop to steal the drug.

The important point about this kind of scenario is not the judgment that is reached, but rather the reasoning process that leads to the judgment.

Kohlberg identified three levels of moral development, each made up of two stages. At the pre-conventional level, notions of right and wrong are determined by authority and the possibility of punishment; and then, at the second stage of this level, by whether an action will likely result in a reward. So, for example, a young child might think Heinz behaved badly because he will probably be caught and punished.

At the conventional level, which most people reach during adolescence, moral reasoning is closely linked to social group membership. At the first stage of this level, a good action is thought to be one that will secure the approval of others; at the second stage, one that is lawful and dutiful.

According to Kohlberg, the third level of moral development, the post-conventional level, is only attained by approximately one-fifth of the population, and is much more abstract in form. For example, moral reasoning at the second stage of this level will invoke universal notions such as justice, the sanctity of life and human dignity. Kohlberg's ideas remain influential today. In a retrospective evaluation of his life and work, Harvard University psychologist, Robert Kegan, noted that the work of three senior members of Harvard's faculty had a direct line to Kohlberg, and that there was no other person, living or dead, about whom that could be said.

Born
1927, Bronxville,
New York

Died
1987, Winthrop,
Massachusetts

I: Preconventional

Law and orde.
Social expectal

III: Postconventional

I: Preconventional

II: Conventional

Postconventional

· Good citizen

· Law and order

· Social expectations

· Good citizen

· Follow rules

punishment

· Acts in own interest.

· Obedience for its own

punishment.

· Acts in own interest.

· Obedience for its own

sake. Autocratic

· Good citizen

· Law and order

· Social expectations

Coercive

Autocratic

Reward

II: Conventional

Task

Accomplishment

Kohlberg proposed a theory of moral development that held that a person's ability to reason morally progresses in stages, only reaching its highest levels of sophistication as adulthood is reached.

2 3 4 5

1950

Solomon Asch *Social Psychology* (1952)

1955

Leon Festinger *A Theory of Cognitive Dissonance* (1957)

1960

Muzafer Sherif *Intergroup Conflict and Cooperation: The Robbers Cave Experiment* (1961)

1965

Henri Tajfel "Experiments in Intergroup Discrimination" (1970)

1970

Philip Zimbardo "The Power and Pathology of Imprisonment" (1971)

Stanley Milgram *Obedience to Authority; An Experimental View* (1974)

1975

The Social Animal

Social psychology, which exploded
onto the psychological stage in
the years immediately after World
War II, looks at how the thoughts
and behavior of individuals are
affected by the presence of other
people. In this section, through the
work and ideas of psychologists
such as Stanley Milgram and Philip
Zimbardo, we look at a number
of socially mediated behaviors,
including obedience, conformity,
scapegoating, and intergroup
conflict.

Social Psychology and the Ignoble Savage

The evolutionary psychologist Steven Pinker has noted that murder, rape, grievous bodily harm, and theft are universal and, thus, found in all human societies. This view contrasts strongly with the philosopher Jean-Jacques Rousseau's "noble savage" concept, which holds that humans are naturally solitary and peaceable. In light of the catastrophic history of the middle part of the twentieth century, it is tempting to dismiss the noble savage idea. However, evidence from the domain of social psychology, which accumulated in the aftermath of the horrors of the extermination camps, suggests a more nuanced, though hardly optimistic, picture.

Social psychology is the branch of the discipline that is concerned with the way our thoughts and behaviors are influenced by other people and by the social context in which we live. Elliot Aronson, one of the world's foremost social psychologists, identifies an 1898 experiment conducted by Norman Triplett that examined how performance is affected by competition as the first social psychological study. Under the rubric of social psychology, psychologists explore phenomena such as conformity, persuasion, obedience, aggression, and prejudice. The evidence from social psychology is not particularly encouraging about the state of humanity. As we'll see in this chapter, Stanley Milgram's experiments showed that under certain conditions, nearly two-thirds of us are willing to torture another human being; Henri Tajfel's research demonstrated that we are willing to discriminate against the members of an out-group even if it is at the expense of our own social group; and Philip Zimbardo's Stanford Prison Experiment showed that given the presence of certain institutional pressures, we are predisposed to engage in hostile and abusive behavior.

> "...it is not so much the kind of person a man is as the kind of situation in which he finds himself that determines how he will act."

–Stanley Milgram

Even if we look at how people form loving relationships there is room for cynicism. For example, a 1972 study by Bernard Murstein, which looked at ninety-nine established couples, found significantly less discrepancy in their attractiveness than in the attractiveness of artificially paired couples. He concluded that "individuals with equal market value for physical attractiveness are more likely to associate in an intimate relationship . . . than individuals with disparate values."

However, there is some ground for optimism in evidence provided by other studies. For example, Muzafer Sherif's work on intergroup conflict demonstrated that intergroup hostility will decrease, and in some circumstances disappear completely, if two disparate groups are required to work together to achieve a shared goal; and Solomon Asch's studies of conformity showed that even under significant pressure to conform, most people, most of the time, do not conform (albeit most people do conform some of the time).

Aronson points out it is wrong to draw the conclusion that people are irremediably terrible because they can be brought to do terrible things. Part of the promise of social psychology is that it will shed light on the sorts of circumstances associated with bad outcomes. As Aronson puts it, we know that some situational variables cause a large majority of "normal" adults to behave badly. Therefore, it is of "paramount importance that we attempt to understand the variables and the processes producing unpleasant or destructive behavior."

The Turkish-born, American-based psychologist Muzafer Sherif is properly regarded as one of the founders of social psychology. He is best known for developing realistic conflict theory, which accounts for the conflict between social groups, and for the prejudice and discrimination that results, in terms of competition for valued goods and resources. His famous Robbers Cave Experiment is taken to provide strong support for the efficacy of this theory.

Sherif and his colleagues started the experiment, which took place in 1954 at a summer camp in Oklahoma, by dividing twenty-two boys—all middle-class, socially well-adjusted, and of above average intelligence—into two groups, which were then kept apart to allow separate group identities to emerge. The two groups, whose members began to refer to themselves as the Rattlers and Eagles, very quickly developed group norms, hierarchies, and an esprit de corps.

Sherif's hypothesis was that if two groups have conflicting aims, their members will become hostile to each other even if the groups are composed of normal, well-adjusted individuals. To test this, the Rattlers and Eagles were introduced, and told they were going to compete against each other in a series of organized games after which one group would be declared the overall winner. The relations between the two groups very rapidly deteriorated once the games began. The Rattlers and the Eagles burned each other's flags, fought, exchanged insults, sent raiding parties to each other's living quarters, and stole from one another.

Rapidly escalating intergroup friction was the clear result of repeatedly bringing the two groups together in competitive and reciprocally frustrating situations. The negative attitudes that each in-group developed toward the out-group resulted in unfavorable stereotypes, which in turn led to name-calling, derogation of the out-group, and the explicit desire to avoid interacting with the out-group. The Robbers Cave Experiment thus provides strong evidence for the proposition that antagonism between social groups is linked to conflicts of interest in relation to valued goods and resources. Sherif also did groundbreaking work on communication, the self, social judgment, and attitude formation and change. At his death, he was generally considered to be one of social psychology's most significant figures.

Born
1906, Ödemis, Turkey

Died
1988, Fairbanks, Alaska

Sherif's famous Robbers Cave Experiment provides strong empirical support for his "realistic conflict theory," which holds that the conflict between social groups is linked to competition for valued goods and resources.

Solomon Asch was one of the twentieth century's great social psychologists. Influenced by the ideas of Gestalt psychology, he conducted important research on spatial orientation, impression formation, and prestige suggestion. He also wrote what was for a long time the discipline's standout textbook, called *Social Psychology* (1952). However, it is for his groundbreaking studies of conformity that he is probably most celebrated.

It was Asch's view that the best measure of conformity is whether a person will agree with other members of a group, who all give the incorrect answer to a question that has an obvious solution. With this in mind, he devised an experimental procedure, now known as the Asch paradigm, to measure the extent of conformity.

An experimental subject is seated with six other people, all of whom are confederates of the experimenter. The experimenter presents two cards to the group, one of which has a single vertical line on it, and the other, a comparison card, three vertical lines labeled A, B, and C. Each person in the group is then asked to say out loud the letter of the comparison line that is the same length as the single vertical line. It is fixed so that the naive subject is always last or last but one to give the answer.

This is done twelve times, but on seven of these occasions—the critical trials—the confederates all give the same wrong answer. The key question is whether the naive subject will conform to the incorrect answer.

The results show significant levels of conformity. Despite the task being easy—mistakes are made less than 1 percent of the time in the absence of pressure to conform—only some 20 percent of subjects give the correct answer on every critical trial; 80 percent conform to the majority on at least one occasion.

After conducting his experiment, Asch would ask naive students why they conformed. The majority said it was because they didn't want to appear stupid in front of their peers, while a minority said they came to the conclusion that the majority must be right. This illustrates the difference between mere compliance—going along with the majority for the sake of appearances—and internalization, where a person's judgments are affected.

Born
1907, Warsaw, Poland

Died
1996, Haverford, Pennsylvania

Asch's famous studies of conformity demonstrate that if it means avoiding social embarrassment, people are willing to conform to the judgments of the majority, even if they know these judgments to be incorrect.

In 1957, a book titled *A Theory of Cognitive Dissonance*, written by Leon Festinger, a young American social psychologist, was published, changing the way that psychologists think about motivation, decision making, and attitude change.

Festinger's cognitive dissonance theory is built on two major claims: first, if a person simultaneously holds two or more conflicting beliefs, this will cause them discomfort; and second, this discomfort functions as a motive to reduce dissonance, which is achieved either by changing one of the beliefs or by introducing a rationalization to explain the conflict.

The phenomenon of cognitive dissonance is often illustrated with reference to a person who smokes cigarettes. If one assumes this person values their own life, then the cognition "I smoke" is inconsistent with the cognition "smoking is potentially lethal." In this situation, a smoker might seek to reduce dissonance by rejecting the evidence that links smoking to cancer, or by denying that longevity is the measure of a good life, or by emphasizing the pleasure that smoking brings.

This example shows how cognitive dissonance can both shape attitudes and undermine our ability to think rationally. This carries with it certain dangers, as another oft cited example will show. Imagine it's come to your attention that a number of people in your workplace believe you have been bullying a subordinate. This results in a conflict between the cognition "I am a good, fair-minded person" and the cognition "people think I'm a bully." In this situation, merely altering your behavior will not straightforwardly eliminate the dissonance, because it leaves both cognitions in place. However, if you tell yourself that your subordinate is incompetent, then you can justify your behavior to yourself—he deserved it—which will result in dissonance reduction. Crucially, this will likely leave the bullying behavior in place, and indeed may well result in it being intensified.

It is hard to overstate the impact of Festinger's original idea. As Elliot Aronson puts it, the theory of cognitive dissonance "has breached the walls of academic psychology and entered the vernacular. 'Cognitive dissonance' is today commonly used by political analysts, TV characters, bloggers, columnists, and comedians."

Born
1919, New York,
New York

Died
1989, New York,
New York

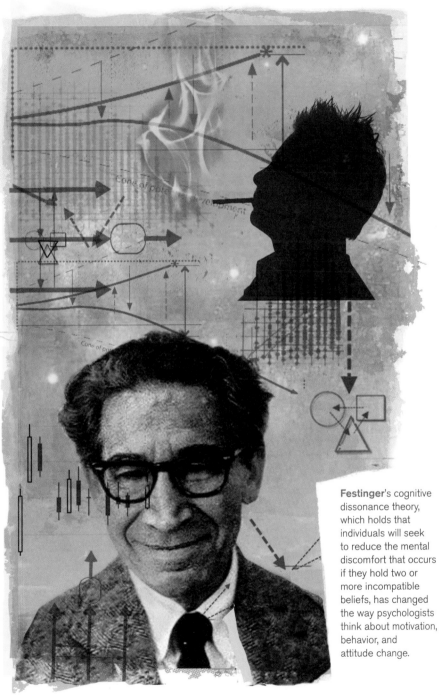

Festinger's cognitive dissonance theory, which holds that individuals will seek to reduce the mental discomfort that occurs if they hold two or more incompatible beliefs, has changed the way psychologists think about motivation, behavior, and attitude change.

Henri Tajfel

Founding Social Identity Theory

The British-based psychologist Henri Tajfel is best known for developing a theory of social identity, which holds that people are predisposed to divide the world up into in-groups and out-groups, defining themselves in terms of their membership of particular in-groups and in opposition to particular out-groups.

Tajfel's groundbreaking minimal group experiments, conducted in the early 1970s, provide strong evidence for this general thesis. An experimental subject is given a trivial task to complete—for example, guessing the number of dots in a cluster—and then directed to a cubicle, where they are told they will be required to allocate "points" to two other people, who will be able to swap the points for money once the experiment is over.

The subject is then informed that they have been assigned to a specific "group" on the basis of how accurately they estimated the number of dots in the cluster. They are also told to which groups the two people to whom they will be required to allocate points/money belong. The subject does not know the identity of these people, has had no contact with them, and knows nothing about them. The idea here is to determine whether this kind of minimal group membership will make a difference to the way that subjects distribute rewards; in other words, will subjects discriminate in favor of the people in their own group and against nongroup members.

Tajfel's results show that this is precisely what they will do. In fact, when offered a choice, subjects seek to maximize the difference between what is allocated to the in-group member and what is allocated to the out-group member, even if this means the in-group member receives less overall than would be available via an alternative strategy.

This is a rather disconcerting result. It shows that even if we don't know the other members of our "group," have never interacted with them, and stand to gain nothing by favoring them, we are still willing to discriminate in favor of in-group members and against out-group members. Although Tajfel's work is not widely known outside the domain of professional psychology, there is no questioning its significance. In 1998, his former students and colleagues published the book *Social Groups and Identities*, as a posthumous tribute to the continuing importance of his work.

Born
1919, Włocławek, Poland

Died
1982, Oxford, England

92

Tajfel's "minimal group" studies have provided support for his theory of social identity, which states that individuals tend to define themselves in terms of their membership of particular in-groups and opposition to particular out-groups.

Philip Zimbardo
Investigating Institutionalized Confinement

In a career lasting more than forty years, the American psychologist Philip Zimbardo has conducted important research on a diverse range of topics, including attitude formation and change, post-traumatic stress syndrome, heroism, and shyness. However, his career has largely been defined by a single study, the Stanford Prison Experiment, which took place in 1971.

The experiment was designed to explore the question of whether prison system brutality is a product of dysfunctional personalities, or whether it is caused, at least in part, by the dehumanizing nature of prison life itself. As Zimbardo put it, the issue at stake was whether people's goodness would triumph over the evil of a prisonlike environment. Zimbardo created his "prison" in the basement of the psychology laboratory at Stanford University and recruited subjects through a newspaper advertisement. Before the study began, he made sure that the chosen participants were psychologically healthy and had had no previous run-ins with the law. His subjects, all students, were randomly allocated to "prison guard" and "prisoner" groups, meaning that both groups were representative of young, white, middle-class America.

The results of the experiment were both stunning and dismaying. It took only a day for the guards to begin to display significant levels of aggression toward the prisoners, with the encounters between the two groups characteristically being "negative, hostile, affrontive, and dehumanizing."

This had a large and disastrous psychological effect on the prisoners. Zimbardo reports that their behavior became passive and "zombie-like," and that as early as the second day, depression, rage, and acute anxiety were all evident. By the time the experiment came to a premature end, after six of a planned fourteen days, five prisoners had been released because of acute psychological suffering, and of the remaining prisoners, only two said they would not be willing to forfeit the money they had earned in return for "parole."

Zimbardo's prison experiment provides strong evidence that social and institutional forces can make good people do horrible things. Although the experiment has been criticized on ethical grounds, it is rightly considered one of the most significant studies in the history of psychology.

Born
1933, New York,
New York

Zimbardo's Stanford Prison Experiment is one of the most significant psychological studies ever conducted, showing that people are predisposed to engage in negative and hostile behavior given the presence of certain institutional and social cues.

The American social psychologist Stanley Milgram is best known for a series of classic experiments on obedience conducted in the early 1960s, which showed that under particular conditions most people are willing to torture another human being.

Milgram's first experiment, now known as the "remote-victim" experiment, had the following setup. Forty male experimental subjects were told they were taking part in a study that was looking at the effects of punishment on learning. Each subject was told they were going to be a "teacher," and they were paired with an experimenter's stooge, who would play the role of "learner." Everything from that point on was scripted, except for the behavior of each subject (i.e., the teacher).

The learner was put into a separate room and wired up to electrodes, through which it seemed an electric shock could be delivered each time an error was made. The teacher was given a small electric shock to convince him that the setup was real (though it wasn't), and then went ahead with the memory test. Each time the learner made a mistake, the teacher was instructed to deliver an electric shock to the learner, with the intensity of the shock increasing by 15 volts for each subsequent mistake.

The extraordinary result of this experiment was that every teacher was willing to deliver a shock of up to 300 volts— labeled "Intense shock" on the machine—despite the fact that it (apparently) caused the learner to pound desperately on the wall. Also, some two-thirds of subjects were willing to give the highest possible shock of 450 volts, even though by this point the learner appeared to be non-responsive.

Milgram found a similar pattern of responses across a total of 18 different experiments, comprising a total of 646 participants (including 40 women, who also showed a 65 percent obedience rate). This led Milgram to conclude that "ordinary people simply doing their jobs, and without any particular hostility on their part, can become agents in a terrible destructive process." Milgram also conducted other important research in a career cut short by his untimely death at the age of fifty-one. In particular, he has been credited with introducing the idea of "six degrees of separation" in his work on social circles.

Born
1933, New York, New York

Died
1984, New York, New York

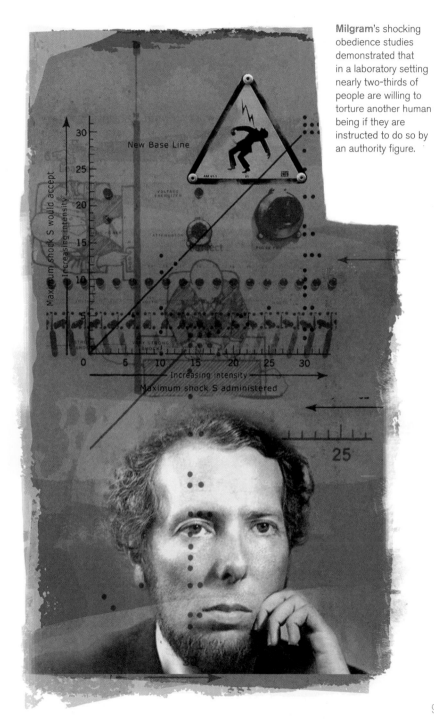

Milgram's shocking obedience studies demonstrated that in a laboratory setting nearly two-thirds of people are willing to torture another human being if they are instructed to do so by an authority figure.

1880	
	Emil Kraepelin *Compendium of Psychiatry* (1883)
	Sigmund Freud *The Interpretation of Dreams* (1899)
1900	
1910	**Alfred Adler** *The Neurotic Constitution* (1912)
1920	**Carl Gustav Jung** *Psychological Types* (1921)
1930	**Melanie Klein** *The Psycho-Analysis of Children* (1932)
1935	**Anna Freud** *Ego and the Mechanisms of Defense* (1936)
	Carl Rogers *Clinical Treatment of the Problem Child* (1939)
1940	**Abraham Maslow** "A Theory of Human Motivation" (1943)
1950	
	Albert Ellis *How to Live with a Neurotic* (1959)
1960	**Thomas Szasz** *The Myth of Mental Illness: Foundations of a Theory of Personal Conduct* (1961)
1965	**Aaron Beck** *The Diagnosis and Management of Depression* (1967)
2012	**Robin Murray** "Criminal Conviction Among Offspring with Parental History of Mental Disorder" (2012)

In Sickness and in Health

Abnormal psychology is the branch of psychology that looks at aberrant patterns of thought and behavior. In this section, we look at the work and thought of psychoanalysts such as Freud and Jung; at the medicalizing of mental illness through the work of clinicians such as Emil Kraepelin; and at the work of humanistic psychologists, such as Abraham Maslow and Carl Rogers, which led to the emergence of client-centered therapeutic techniques.

The Medical Model and Its Discontents

The medical model asserts that certain patterns of abnormal behavior are best viewed as illnesses. The significance of this idea for the way we view phenomena such as depression and bipolar disorder is clear in the terminology we routinely employ: mental illness, mental disorder, and psychopathology.

It is possible to get a good idea of what's involved in the medical model by looking at how modern psychiatry views schizophrenia, the most severe of the common mental disorders. The term "schizophrenia" roughly translates as "split mind." However, this etymology is somewhat misleading, because the illness has little in common with conditions such as multiple personality disorder. In fact, people with schizophrenia suffer a severely distorted perception of reality, which includes disordered thinking, delusions, and, above all, auditory and non-auditory hallucinations.

The standard view among psychiatrists is that the symptoms that lead to a diagnosis of schizophrenia are, at least in part, caused by brain dysfunction. The dopamine hypothesis suggests that the disorder is linked to an excess of dopamine transmission, particularly in the mesolimbic system of the brain. There is plenty of evidence to support this hypothesis. For example, all antipsychotic drugs work by blocking dopamine, and all drugs that increase dopamine can cause psychosis.

However, this medical view that schizophrenia is an illness with an underlying pathology is by no means universally endorsed. Some radical critics of psychiatry, such as Thomas Szasz, have suggested that schizophrenia and, more generally, mental illness simply do not exist. Roughly, their argument is that people are labeled as suffering from a disorder like schizophrenia in order to "control" and

> *"We have no enemy whom we can fight, exorcise, or dispel by `cure.' What we do have are problems in living..."*

> —Thomas Szasz

"neutralize" behavior that is deemed to be socially unacceptable. As we'll see later in this chapter, Szasz argues that the notion of a "mental illness" is a contradiction in terms: the mind is a non-material, non-spatial entity, so, therefore, cannot be subject to the pathological changes in physiology that constitute illness.

The validity of the medical model is further called into question when one considers other mental disorders. For example, Albert Ellis, founder of rational emotive behavior therapy, did not look for the causes of depression in an underlying brain illness but, instead, identified a number of irrational beliefs that were characteristically held by depressed people, which resulted in them viewing the world in a negative way. In these terms, therapy should not be targeted toward the brain, as would be the case if antidepressant drugs were prescribed, but rather toward challenging the irrational beliefs that result in negative perceptions and judgments.

There is no doubt the original impulse for the medical model was good. Not least, naturalizing disorders such as schizophrenia functioned to strip them of their quasi-religious baggage—so, for example, in the West at least, hearing voices is no longer seen as a sign of witchcraft. There is also persuasive empirical evidence to suggest that identifiable physiological risk factors exist for disorders such as bipolar disorder and depression. However, the extent to which it is appropriate to label disorders that are in effect "problems in living" as "illnesses" remains an open question.

Emil Kraepelin

Systematizing Categories of Mental Illness

The German psychiatrist Emil Kraepelin has a strong claim to be considered the founder of scientific psychiatry. In particular, the modern systems of psychiatric classification are based on the Kraepelinian view that mental disorders are distinct entities, each with its own cause, symptoms, course, and terminus. Kraepelin is also notable for having written the modern era's first widely read textbook of psychiatry.

Kraepelin argued that psychiatry could only put itself on a scientific footing by conducting a systematic survey of the patterns of symptoms that occur in the presence of mental distress. This, he thought, was necessary in order to identify the boundaries of specific disease manifestations, the first stage in the process of uncovering their underlying physiological pathology. On the basis of thousands of observations, Kraepelin identified two broad categories of mental disorder; dementia praecox (now known as schizophrenia), and manic-depressive psychosis (now known as bipolar disorder).

Dementia praecox (literally, "early dementia") has a number of characteristic symptoms, the most important of which is auditory hallucinations. Disordered thought is also common, as is the sense that thoughts are being controlled or influenced by outside sources. Kraepelin had a largely pessimistic view of dementia praecox, noting that complete recovery rarely occurs.

Manic-depressive psychosis, which is characterized by alternating episodes of mania and depression, is hard to distinguish from dementia praecox in its acute phase, but is associated with a better outcome. Symptoms of mania include racing and disordered thought, elevated mood, ideas of greatness, increased sexual appetite, and weight gain; symptoms of depression include torpor, slowed speech, an inability to act, feelings of guilt, and weight loss.

The similarity of Kraepelin's conceptions of dementia praecox and manic-depressive psychosis to their modern equivalents—schizophrenia and bipolar disorder—is striking, and testament both to the care he took in his observations and to the impact of his work on the development of modern psychiatry.

Born
1856, Neustrelitz, Germany

Died
1926, Munich, Germany

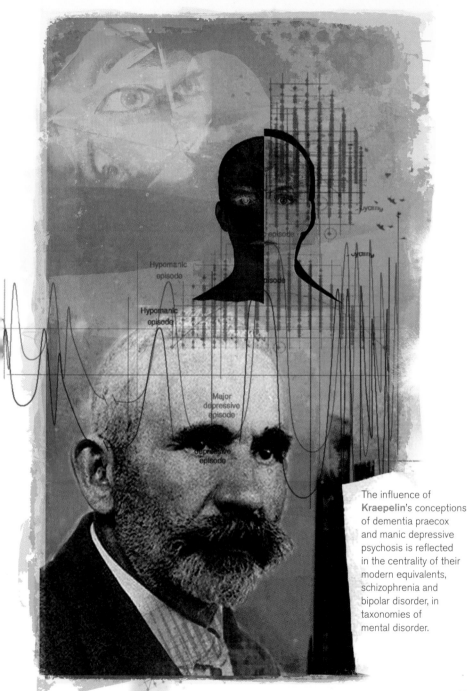

The influence of **Kraepelin**'s conceptions of dementia praecox and manic depressive psychosis is reflected in the centrality of their modern equivalents, schizophrenia and bipolar disorder, in taxonomies of mental disorder.

Sigmund Freud
Founding Psychoanalysis

It would be hard to overestimate the influence of the ideas of Sigmund Freud, the father of psychoanalysis, on twentieth century thought. More than anybody else, he is responsible for undermining the view that human beings are rational decision makers, masters of their own minds and destiny.

Freud argued that the human psyche is divided into three distinct parts: the id, which comprises a person's instincts, primarily their libidinal instincts; the ego, which is the rational, decision-making aspect of the psyche; and the superego, which is the judgmental, censorious part. The id seeks the immediate gratification of its desires. However, governed by a reality principle, the ego is required to balance the demands of the id against the requirements of living in the world. At the same time, the ego has to manage the superego, ensuring that thoughts and behavior fall within limits that are morally acceptable from the point of view of the superego.

This situation is replete with the potential for psychic conflict. A hypervigilant superego, for example, will result in guilt, anxiety, and burial of unwanted desires and memories within the unconscious. Freud claimed that these sorts of repressed conflicts have a dynamic character. Inevitably, they make their presence felt in conscious life, through dreams, slips of the tongue (parapraxes), phobias, and fantasy. In a famous case study, Freud argued that the fear of horses experienced by his patient Little Hans was in fact a manifestation of his fear of his father, which was rooted in an Oedipal desire—that is, a sexual desire—for his mother, and the fact that his father was therefore a kind of love rival.

According to Freud, it is the job of the psychoanalyst to decode the messages that the unconscious sends to the conscious mind. The analyst will make use of techniques such as free association, word association, and dream analysis in order to bring repressed memories to the surface. By knowing the unconscious roots of our thoughts and behavior, we will be in a better position to control them.

The history of ideas of the twentieth century would have been entirely different had Freud not lived. Although there are many question marks concerning the validity of his ideas, there is no doubting his intellectual and cultural significance.

Born
1856, Príbor, Czech Republic

Died
1939, London, England

Freud's psychoanalytic theory, and in particular his tripartite conception of the human psyche, played a central role in the twentieth century in undermining the idea that human beings are rational social actors.

Alfred Adler, the founder of Individual Psychology and one-time colleague of Sigmund Freud, is perhaps best known in the present day as the originator of psychological concepts such as "overcompensation" and "the inferiority complex."

Adler first outlined his ideas about compensation in his book, *A Study of Organic Inferiority and Its Psychical Compensation*, published in 1907. In essence, his argument was that the existence of a physiological defect—for example, deafness—will often result in a compensatory impulse that will lead an individual to excel in precisely the area most relevant to their handicap. So, for example, he noted that the ancient Greek statesman Demosthenes stuttered as a youth, but overcame this problem to become a great orator; and that the champion Finnish athlete, Paavo Nurmi, limped as a child.

In his later work, Adler extended this idea so that it did not require the existence of a physiological defect. He argued that all children experience feelings of inferiority. These might be particularly pronounced in the case of a neglected, or abused, child, but even in the best circumstances, a child will feel small and helpless in the face of the adult world. The consequence is that from an early age, children are striving for power and superiority in order to compensate for these feelings of inferiority.

The neurotic response to this situation will see the child withdrawing from the world, thereby avoiding those situations that threaten to bring to light their perceived inferiority. If this is not resolved going into adulthood, then an Inferiority Complex is the likely consequence. This typically involves the adult setting impossible to accomplish "fictive goals," and then explaining their failure to meet these goals in terms of the symptoms of their neurotic state.

Adler did not believe that a feeling of inferiority is pathological in itself. In fact, it is a normal part of development for individuals to strive for power and superiority. However, this striving must be realistic in terms of the challenges of society, work, and sex, otherwise the risk of overcompensation—for example, the weak man who becomes a bully—or a retreat into neurotic illness looms large.

Born
1870, Rudolfsheim, Austria

Died
1937, Aberdeen, Scotland

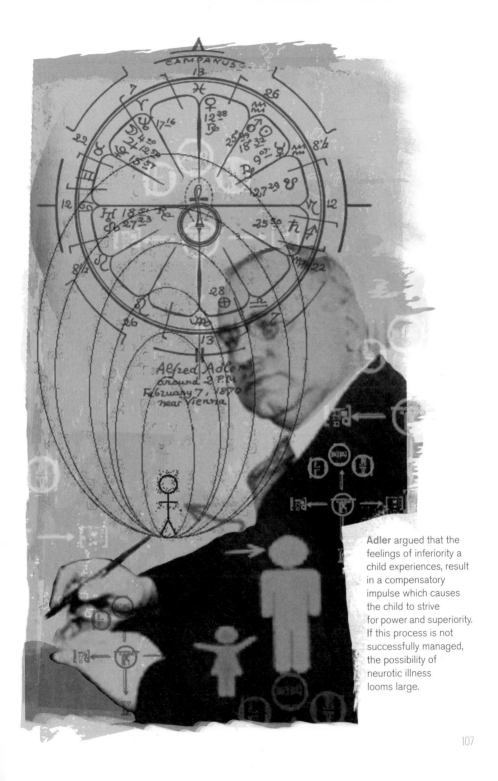

Adler argued that the feelings of inferiority a child experiences, result in a compensatory impulse which causes the child to strive for power and superiority. If this process is not successfully managed, the possibility of neurotic illness looms large.

Carl Gustav Jung, the Swiss psychotherapist and founder of analytical psychology, was at one time a close friend and colleague of Sigmund Freud; however, in 1913, their friendship came to an end, in part because Jung wanted to take psychoanalytic theory in a direction that Freud had not envisaged. In particular, Jung denied that the libido is entirely sexual in character, and, therefore, contrary to Freudian orthodoxy, he believed that there was more to neurosis than simply the existence of unconscious sexual conflicts.

According to Jung, the psyche is split into three interacting parts: consciousness; the personal unconscious; and the collective unconscious. The conscious mind is the part of the psyche that is directly known to the person. Jung identified two personality types that determine how an individual is oriented toward the world. The extrovert directs libidinal energies outward toward the external world; the introvert looks inward, focusing on subjective feelings and experience. It was Jung's belief that most individuals will stay true to their personality type throughout their life.

Jung's treatment of the unconscious aspects of the psyche, and particularly his idea of the collective unconscious, was unorthodox. He argued that humans are wired up to experience and orient themselves toward the world in the same way as their ancestors did. The innate organizing principles of the collective unconscious are termed "archetypes." Examples include: the persona—the face we present to the world; the shadow—the source of our animal instincts; the self—the organizing principle by means of which we structure our personality; the anima— the feminine in the masculine; and the animus—the masculine in the feminine.

Although this notion of the collective unconscious is the most novel aspect of Jung's approach, it is also the most problematic. His critics contend, with some justification, that it has more in common with mythology than with scientific theory.

Jung's ideas certainly represent an interesting variation on the theme of Freudian psychoanalysis, and there is no doubting the influence of his formulations. However, the extent to which his ideas are justified by what we know about the world is questionable. This is the general case with psychoanalytic theory.

Born
1875, Kesswil,
Switzerland

Died
1961, Zurich,
Switzerland

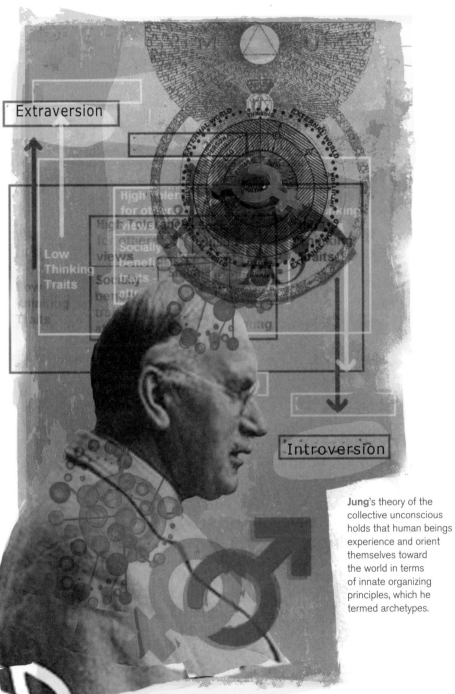

Extraversion

Low Thinking Traits

Introversion

Jung's theory of the collective unconscious holds that human beings experience and orient themselves toward the world in terms of innate organizing principles, which he termed archetypes.

Melanie Klein was one of the pioneering figures of psychoanalysis, responsible for advances in both clinical practice and psychoanalytic theory. In particular, she devised a method for analyzing the play of children, which made it possible for psychoanalytic techniques to be applied to infants as young as two years old; and on the theoretical side, she developed an alternative treatment of the origins of the Freudian superego, and elaborated concepts such as the paranoid-schizoid position and the depressive position that are now part of the psychoanalytic lexicon.

According to orthodox Freudian theory, the superego develops with the resolution of the Oedipus complex at about four years of age. Klein rejected this view, arguing instead that its origins can be found much earlier, in the first months of life.

The earliest stages of an infant's psychic life are characterized by the existence of two major developmental phases: the paranoid-schizoid position and the depressive position. Klein's famous distinction between "good breast" and "bad breast" will shed some light on the character of the paranoid-schizoid position.

In the first stages of life, an infant makes no distinction between their own ego and the objects of the outside world. This means that whenever feelings of love and hatred are experienced, they are projected into the outside world, with the consequence that the objects of the world take on the guise of these emotions. Thus, Klein argued that "the earliest experiences of the infant are split between wholly good ones with 'good' objects and wholly bad experiences with 'bad' objects."

The infant's first object is the mother's breast, which is sometimes rewarding (when it supplies plentiful milk) and sometimes not (when it doesn't satisfy the infant's needs). The consequence is that the infant will split their feelings of love and hatred, and project them onto a single object (the breast), thereby dividing it into two: the good breast (or mother) is loved and felt to be nourishing; the bad breast (or mother) is hated and felt to be persecutory.

The fact that the emotions of love and hate function in this all or nothing way means that the infant's world during these early months is "peopled by gods and devils—a world which appears sometimes a heaven and at other times a very hell" (J.A.C. Brown).

Born
1882, Vienna, Austria

Died
1960, London, England

Klein argued that the newly born infant experiences the world in a radically divided way, with the objects of its experience being split into those that are wholly good and those that are wholly bad.

Good

Contrariety

Bad

Anna Freud, Sigmund Freud's youngest daughter, was a renowned clinical psychoanalyst in her own right, pioneering the practice of child psychoanalysis and making important contributions to psychoanalytic theory, particularly in relation to what is known as "ego psychology," the branch of psychoanalysis that focuses on the normal and pathological development of the ego or conscious mind.

In her most important work, *Ego and the Mechanisms of Defense*, she examines the way that the ego defends itself against the "painful or unendurable ideas or affects" that exist as a result of tensions between the clamors of the id (the instinctual part of the personality), the demands of the outside world, and the prohibitions of the superego (the moral, censorious part of the psyche).

She identifies five novel defense mechanisms: denial in fantasy, denial in word and act, restriction of the ego, identification with the aggressor, and altruism. Denial in fantasy refers to the process of managing a painful fact or situation by imaginatively transforming it into its opposite. Denial in word and deed similarly refers to the process of denying some aspect of the world, only this time through words and actions (for example, "I am as strong as Daddy").

Restriction of the ego is illustrated by the case of the small boy who refuses to play football with his friends because he recognizes their superior skills and fears humiliation. His reluctance to play the game then extends into a general dislike for the game and a disdain for those people who choose to play and follow it. Identification with the aggressor is a method of dealing with anxiety that relies on adopting the characteristics of the oppressor, thereby transforming oneself into the powerful figure. Thus, for example, the boy bullied at home by his father will himself bully weaker children at school.

Altruism functions as a defense mechanism by allowing the cathartic fulfillment of desire by the surrender of one's own wishes to another person. Anna Freud points to the example of Cyrano de Bergerac, who helps a rival win the affections of the woman he himself loves because he believes his own ugliness denies him "the dream of being loved."

Born
1895, Vienna, Austria

Died
1982, London, England

Anna Freud
identified ego defense mechanisms, such as denial in fantasy and restriction of the ego, which function to protect the ego against the conflict between the id and the superego, which lies at the heart of the psyche.

The American psychologist Carl Rogers was one of the early pioneers of the humanistic approach to psychology, and the driving force behind the development of client-centered psychotherapy. He was also nominated for the Nobel Peace Prize in 1987 for his work on intergroup conflict in Northern Ireland and South Africa.

At the center of Rogers' approach is the concept of "the self," which refers to an "organized, consistent set of perceptions and beliefs about oneself." Put simply, the self, or self-concept, is the mental picture that a person has of themselves. If this picture is reasonably accurate, if it is congruent with reality, then it will fit well with actual experience. However, if it is not, if it is incongruent with reality, then the lack of fit between self-concept and actual experience can lead to psychological difficulties.

According to Rogers, incongruent experiences threaten the integrity of a person's self-concept, and therefore provoke anxiety. The typical response is to employ defense mechanisms in order to deal with the incongruence. For example, a young woman who considers herself unattractive, but is asked to a dance by an attractive man, might explain away the incongruence by telling herself that he only feels sorry for her, or that it is a joke. In this way, she protects her self-concept, but only at the expense of denying herself a potentially positive experience.

Rogers advocated client-centered therapy as the means to deal with incongruence. This relies on what he called unconditional positive regard. The therapist provides complete acceptance and nonjudgmental support of the client as a person in a setting that is genuinely emotionally supportive and engaged. The aim is to allow the client to come to terms with thoughts and feelings they would otherwise deny as being their own, thereby enabling them to develop a more realistic self-concept.

Rogers believed that everybody has the capacity to fulfill their potential as a human being. However, this is not an easy thing to achieve: "It involves the stretching and growing of becoming more and more of one's potentialities. It involves the courage to be. It means launching oneself fully into the stream of life."

Born
1902, Oak Park, Ilinois

Died
1987, San Diego, California

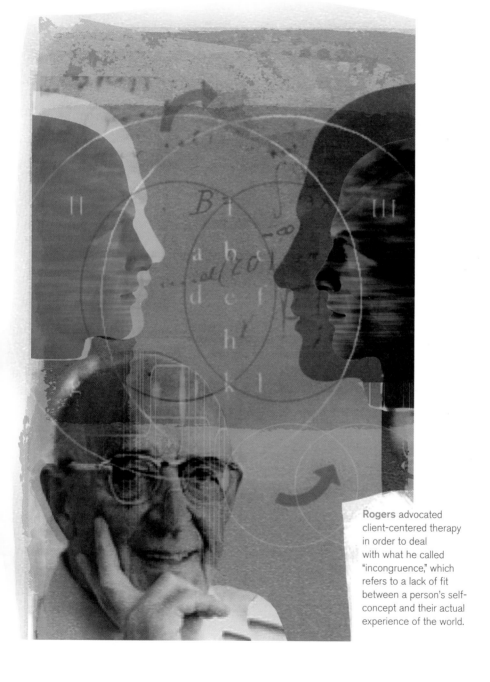

Rogers advocated client-centered therapy in order to deal with what he called "incongruence," which refers to a lack of fit between a person's self-concept and their actual experience of the world.

The American psychologist Abraham H. Maslow was one of the most important figures in the humanistic psychology movement that emerged in the United States in the middle part of the twentieth century. The humanistic approach, in contrast to behaviorism and psychoanalysis, emphasizes the importance of human experience, the potential for personal growth and the possibility of self-fulfillment.

According to Maslow, human motivation can be understood in terms of a pyramidal hierarchy of needs. At the bottom, there are basic physiological needs; then come higher level needs, including safety needs, the need for love and belonging, and the need for esteem. At the top there is the need for self-actualization, which refers to the possibility of realizing one's full potential, or "becoming everything that one is capable of becoming."

Normally, needs at the bottom must be satisfied before higher level needs come into play. For example, a starving person will not be concerned with their need for esteem until their hunger has been satisfied. At the higher levels, needs are not merely a matter of satisfying biological imperatives, but rather are dependent upon living life in a certain kind of way, and, therefore, they are much harder to satisfy.

Even though everybody is capable of self-actualization, most people do not achieve it. Maslow identified William James, Albert Einstein, and Abraham Lincoln as example of self-actualizers, arguing that they had in common that they were spontaneous in action and thought, able to perceive reality accurately, happy to tolerate uncertainty, creative, interested in problem solving, and able to enjoy deep relationships with just a small number of people. Maslow also noted that self-actualizers seem to have many peak experiences in their lives. These are moments of extreme happiness and fulfillment, which often involve a loss of the sense of self, and which will sometimes result in positive changes to a person's behavior.

It not yet clear whether the kinds of ideas pioneered by Maslow have been particularly effective in helping people to achieve psychological health. However, humanistic psychology has been an important corrective to the scientism of behaviorist psychology and the reductionism of psychoanalysis.

Born
1908, Brooklyn, New York

Died
1970, Menlo Park, California

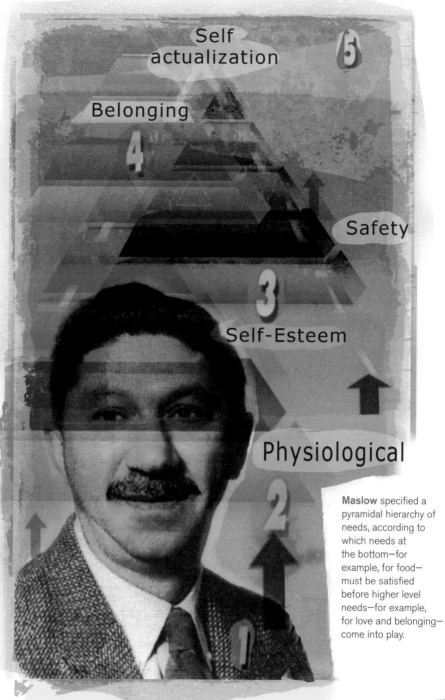

Self actualization

Belonging

Safety

Self-Esteem

Physiological

Maslow specified a pyramidal hierarchy of needs, according to which needs at the bottom—for example, for food—must be satisfied before higher level needs—for example, for love and belonging—come into play.

The American psychologist Albert Ellis spent the early part of his career committed to the methods of psychoanalysis as the deepest and most effective form of therapy. However, his confidence in the technique evaporated at the beginning of the 1950s, which led him to develop Rational Emotive Behavioral Therapy (REBT), the therapeutic approach for which he is now celebrated.

REBT holds that psychological problems arise from irrational judgments and interpretations; from inappropriate emotional reactions to unexceptional stimuli; and from habitually dysfunctional patterns of behavior.

According to Ellis, if something unpleasant occurs in a person's life, they are confronted with a choice: they can either be healthily and self-helpingly frustrated, disappointed and annoyed; or they can be unhealthily and self-defeatingly inconsolable, terrified and panicked. Normally, the healthy response is engendered by rational beliefs and the unhealthy response by irrational or self-defeating beliefs.

Ellis identified a number of irrational and self-defeating beliefs that are common in Western and other cultures. These include, for example: "I must be loved and accepted by absolutely everybody"; "I must always be excellent and never make mistakes, otherwise I'm worthless"; "I must damn others if they behave in ways I consider wicked"; and "I must live in favorable and happy circumstances, otherwise things will be so awful I won't be able to bear it." More generally, Ellis argued that when people take their strong desire for love, success, and comfort, and turn it into a series of musts, needs, and imperatives, then it is likely they will end up anxious, depressed, and self-pitying.

The goal of REBT is to challenge people's irrational and self-defeating ideas and beliefs. Therefore, effective therapists not only listen carefully to their clients, and provide unconditional acceptance whatever their clients' particular circumstances, but they also show them how and why their thinking goes wrong, and what they can do to change their thoughts and behavior patterns in a way that will lessen their psychological distress. In this sense, REBT is a much more active-directive therapy than more traditional psychotherapies, which, according to Ellis, accounts for its greater effectiveness.

Born
1913, Pittsburgh, Pennsylvania

Died
2007, New York, New York

Ellis developed Rational Emotive Behavioral Therapy, which holds that psychological problems are a function of irrational judgments and interpretations, and that these can be successfully challenged within the context of therapy.

In the late 1950s, the Hungarian-born, American-based psychiatrist Thomas Szasz wrote a number of articles critical of the practice of psychiatry, arguing in one that the notion of mental illness had no more validity as an explanation of behavior than the claim that a person had been possessed by the devil. These articles were a prelude to the publication of his seminal work, *The Myth of Mental Illness*, which can be seen as an attempt to demolish the conceptual foundations of psychiatry.

According to Szasz, the claim that mental illnesses are diagnosable brain disorders is either a lie or a naive error. The concept of "illness" requires the presence of a pathological change in cells, tissues, and organs, which is clearly impossible in the case of a non-spatial, non-material entity such as the mind. It follows that the idea of "mental illness" is merely a metaphor, and "minds can be 'sick' only in the sense that jokes are 'sick' or economies are 'sick.'" Szasz did not deny that, in some cases, the symptoms of "mental illness" are caused by the presence of an organic brain disease (as in the case of Alzheimer's disease, for example). However, in these cases, the patient doesn't have a mental illness at all, they have a physical illness, and to claim otherwise is simply to misdiagnose them.

Szasz argued that in the vast majority of cases of "mental illness," there is no underlying brain disease. Rather, what is being diagnosed as "mental illness" are "problems in living," forms of behavior that deviate from what society considers to be acceptable. In this sense, a diagnosis of "mental illness" is an attempt to control behavior that is potentially threatening to the social order. Thus, he insisted that "mental hospitals are like prisons, not hospitals; that involuntary mental hospitalization is a type of imprisonment, not medical care; and that coercive psychiatrists function as judges and jailers, not healers."

Szasz accepted that the behavior patterns that psychiatrists identify as indicative of mental illness are often strange, unnerving, and annoying. They may also be upsetting to the person involved. But, in almost all cases, they are not a symptom of a brain disorder.

Born
1920, Budapest, Hungary

Died
2012, Manlius, New York

Szasz is famous for arguing that mental illness is a myth, and that psychiatrists in fact diagnose "problems in living," forms of behavior that deviate from what society considers to be acceptable.

The American psychiatrist Aaron Beck is best known as the originator of cognitive therapy, an approach widely used in the treatment of clinical depression that stresses the importance of the way that individuals view themselves and the world around them for an understanding of the condition.

Beck's crucial insight was that patients who are depressed view many of their circumstances in an unrealistically negative light, and that it is the constant repetition of negative thoughts that keeps painful emotions and problematic behaviors in place.

His cognitive triad specifies three types of negative thoughts that are common in depression: thoughts about the self, the world, and the future. People suffering from depression often see themselves as useless or hopeless, and view the world as unfriendly, hostile and alien, confronting them with insurmountable barriers and obstacles. They see no way out of their situation and view the future through a prism of hopelessness.

Beck argues that the automatic negative thoughts characteristic of depression arise from a number of typical cognitive biases, including, for example, black and white thinking, and arbitrary inference. Black and white thinking is most commonly associated with the setting of impossible goals, which, when not met, result in an inappropriately negative judgment. For example, an athlete trains hard to run a marathon, but aims for a hugely unlikely time, and then is highly critical of himself when he fails to meet his target.

Arbitrary inference occurs when an individual draws an inappropriately negative conclusion on the basis of insufficient or absent evidence. For example, a woman concludes that she is hopeless because she happens to wear the same dress to a party as a friend.

Cognitive therapy aims to challenge these sorts of negative thoughts and cognitive biases. With the help of a therapist, clients are taught how to subject their judgments to reality testing. In this way, the hope is they will come to see just how inappropriately negative their thoughts actually are.

Born
1921, Providence,
Rhode Island

Beck is the originator of cognitive therapy, a therapeutic technique that emphasizes the importance of negative thoughts in the emergence of disorders and seeks to challenge these thoughts in a therapeutic setting.

The Scottish psychiatrist Sir Robin Murray earned his reputation as one of the world's top psychiatrists primarily through his work with schizophrenia patients. Together with his colleagues, he originated and developed the idea that schizophrenia is at least in part a neurodevelopmental disorder.

The orthodox view about schizophrenia used to be that it is a degenerative disorder. The brain of a schizophrenia sufferer starts off normal, but something happens to it during their teens or twenties, and then it deteriorates.

Murray's idea is different. He proposes that the brains of people with schizophrenia have developed in subtly deviant ways. Put simply, something has happened to the wiring of the brain—perhaps for reasons to do with genetics or early environmental insult—that makes the schizophrenia sufferer more vulnerable to hallucinations and delusions. It is important to be clear about what Murray is claiming here. It is *not* that particular developmental problems lead inevitably to schizophrenia. Rather, it is that under certain circumstances, neural systems develop in a way that makes the occurrence of schizophrenia more likely. In particular, subtle developmental changes leave people much more vulnerable to the effects of stressful events in their lives.

Murray's work with Afro-Caribbean patients sheds light on the complexity of the causal factors that result in schizophrenia. He found that rates of schizophrenia among people of Afro-Caribbean origin living in the UK are six times higher than among the white population in the UK, and, crucially, six times higher than among the black population living in the West Indies. This suggests that if these patients had still been living in the West Indies, they would have been far less likely to have developed the illness. Murray suggests that there is something about the adversity in the lives of this group of people that explains the much higher incidence rate.

Additionally, although schizophrenia is associated with certain characteristic symptoms—in particular, hallucinations—this does not mean that the same biological cause is always in play. Thus, Murray argues that it is entirely possible that people get schizophrenia for a mixture of different reasons.

Born
1944, Glasgow, Scotland

Murray earned his reputation as one of the world's top psychiatrists for developing the view that schizophrenia is a neurodevelopmental disorder and that it emerges in the presence of a complex network of biological and social factors.

Glossary

Abnormal psychology: The domain of psychology that focuses on abnormal behavior and the causes of mental distress.

Behaviorism: An approach to psychology that holds that the discipline must focus solely upon observable behavior.

Classical conditioning: A form of learning discovered by Ivan Pavlov that relies on pairing an unconditioned stimulus with a neutral stimulus in order to create a conditioned stimulus that will provoke a conditioned response.

Cognitive dissonance: Now known as edema, it is a feeling of distress that occurs when a person finds themself holding two contradictory beliefs (for example, "I'm a bully," "I'm a nice person").

Cognitive psychology: An approach to psychology that focuses on internal mental processes, and treats the brain (and mind) as if it were akin to an information processing system.

Conformity: A change in behavior or thought that occurs under the pressure of social influence, normally to allow a person to fit in with a particular group.

Corpus callosum: The thick bundle of nerves that connects the brain's two hemispheres.

Developmental psychology: The domain of psychology that looks at the changes in thought and behavior that occur over the lifespan of an individual.

Empirical evidence: Data which is derived from observation and measurement, and therefore, in principle, can be verified by a community of peers.

Eugenics: The science, pioneered by Francis Galton, that aims to improve the genetic stock of the human species by means of selective breeding.

Experimental subject: The human subjects of an experiment (so, for example, if you're testing memory, then the person whose memory you are testing is the experimental subject).

Factor analysis: A statistical technique that reduces a large number of factors to a smaller number of dimensions by looking for correlations between the original factors.

Humanistic psychology: An approach to psychology that emphasizes the importance of human experience, the potential for personal growth, and the possibility of self-fulfillment.

Iconic memory: A fast-decaying store of visual information that is accessible for processing, but only for a very brief period of time.

Inferiority: The feeling, often unwarranted, that one is inadequate, not measuring up to society's standards across particular dimensions (for example, moral, social, intellectual).

Intentionality: The directedness of consciousness; consciousness is always consciousness of something.

Introspection: The technique of directing one's own attention to the contents of one's own mind.

Law of effect: The principle, discovered by Edward Thorndike, that if a behavior results in satisfaction, then that behavior is strengthened (that is, it is more likely to occur).

Limited capacity channel: The brain is a limited capacity channel in the sense that there is an upper limit on the amount of incoming information that it is able to process (which means that information has to be filtered).

Materialism: The view that the only thing that exists is physical matter, and that all phenomena, including consciousness, are ultimately reducible to matter.

Multivariate analysis: A general term for statistical techniques that analyze the relationships between multiple variables.

Operant conditioning: A form of learning where behavior is modified by consequences that are either reinforcing or punishing.

Psyche: The totality of the human mind, both conscious and unconscious (this term is often used in the context of psychoanalytic theory).

Psychoanalysis: A therapeutic approach, originated by Sigmund Freud, which holds that mental disturbances such as neurosis, depression, and anxiety are a function of unresolved conflicts that exist in the unconscious parts of the psyche.

Social psychology: The domain of psychology that looks at how thought and behavior is influenced by the presence of other people.

Split-brain patients: Patients who have had their corpus callosum severed, thereby making it impossible for information to pass between the two brain hemispheres.

Index